KEY CASES

LAND

LAW

2009–2010 EDITION

JUDITH BRAY

HODDER
EDUCATION
AN HACHETTE UK COMPANY

Orders: please contact Bookpoint Ltd, 130 Milton Park, Abingdon, Oxon OX14 4SB. Telephone: (44) 01235 827720. Fax: (44) 01235 400454. Lines are open from 9.00 – 5.00, Monday to Saturday, with a 24 hour message answering service. You can also order through our website www.hoddereducation.co.uk

If you have any comments to make about this, or any of our other titles, please send them to educationenquiries@hodder.co.uk

British Library Cataloguing in Publication Data
A catalogue record for this title is available from the British Library

ISBN 978 1 444 104868

First edition published 2006
Second edition publishd 2009
Impression number   10 9 8 7 6 5 4 3 2
Year   2014 2013 2012 2011

Hachette UK's policy is to use papers that are natural, renewable and recyclable products and made fromwood grown in sustainable forests. The logging and manufacturing processes are expected to conform to the environmental regulations of the country of origin.

Typeset by Transet Limited, Coventry, England.
Printed in Great Britain for Hodder Education, an Hachette UK Company, 338 Euston Road, London NW1 3BH by CPI Cox & Wyman Ltd., Reading, Berkshire RG1 8EX.

CONTENTS

TABLE OF CASES   vi

PREFACE   xi

Chapter 1   THE DEFINITION OF 'LAND'

1.1   The definition of 'land'   2
1.2   Ownership below the surface of land   5
1.3   Items found in and on land   5
1.4   Fixtures and fittings   11

Chapter 2   TRANSFER AND CREATION OF RIGHTS IN LAND

2.1   Rights prior to exchange of contracts   18
2.2   Avoidance of the strict formalities of transfer   20
2.3   The effect in law of exchange of contracts   22

Chapter 3   UNREGISTERED LAND   23

Chapter 4   REGISTERED LAND

4.1   Personal rights cannot bind third parties and
      cannot be overriding   29
4.2   Overriding rights   30
4.3   Unregistered rights in registered land existing as
      constructive trusts   36

Chapter 5   EQUITABLE RIGHTS IN LAND: RESULTING AND CONSTRUCTIVE TRUSTS

5.1   Resulting trusts   39
5.2   Constructive trusts   47
5.3   Assessing the shares in resulting and constructive trusts 54

Chapter 6   PROPRIETARY ESTOPPEL

6.1	Definition	61
6.2	The representation	62
6.3	Reliance on the representation	65
6.4	Detrimental reliance	66
6.5	The remedy in estoppel	68

Chapter 7   LICENCES

| 7.1 | Types of licence | 72 |
| 7.2 | The effect of licences on third parties | 76 |

Chapter 8   CO-OWNERSHIP

8.1	Express declaration of trust of co-owned land	82
8.2	Severance under statute	83
8.3	Severance by post	84
8.4	Severance under common law	87
8.5	Forfeiture	89

Chapter 9   TRUSTS OF LAND

9.1	The effect of a trust over land	92
9.2	The purpose of the trust	93
9.3	Sale under the Trusts of Land and Appointment of Trustees Act 1996	95
9.4	Other applications under the Trusts of Land and Appointment of Trustees Act 1996	96
9.5	Repairs by a co-trustee and the payment of rent	97
9.6	Applications to sell trust property in bankruptcy	99
9.7	The effect of overreaching	101

Chapter 10   EASEMENTS

10.1	Characteristics of an easement	104
10.2	The grant of an easement	110
10.3	Prescription	114
10.4	Excessive use	115

Chapter 11   COVENANTS

11.1	The nature of covenants	118
11.2	Covenants at law	120
11.3	Covenants in equity	122
11.4	Building schemes	125
11.5	Remedies for breach of a restrictive covenant	127

Chapter 12   MORTGAGES

12.1	Rights of the mortgagor	130
12.2	Rights of the mortgagee	140

Chapter 13   LEASES

13.1	The nature of a lease	149
13.2	The difference between a lease and a licence	150
13.3	Key features of a lease	151
13.4	Remedies	155

Chapter 14   ADVERSE POSSESSION

14.1	Meaning of 'adverse possession'	159
14.2	Factual possession	159
14.3	Intention to possess	160
14.4	Adverse possession of leasehold property	164
14.5	Human rights	164

Index   **167**

TABLE OF CASES

KEY CASES – LAND LAW – TABLE OF CASES

88 Berkeley Road [1971] Ch 648 ....81, 85

A-G Securities v Vaughan [1990] 1 AC 417 ....148, 155
AIB Finance v Debtors AC [1998] 2 All ER 929 ....130, 145
Abbey National v Cann [1991] 1 AC 56 ....28, 33
Abbott v Abbott [2008] 1 FLR 1451, PC...46, 47
Alliance & Leicester plc v Slayford [2001] 1 All ER (Comm) 1 ....129, 140
Antoniades v Villiers [1990] 1 AC 417 ....148, 154
Armory v Delamirie (1722) 1 Strange 505 (93 ER 664)..1, 5
Ashburn Anstalt v Arnold [1989] Ch 1 ....71, 79, 80, 148, 152
Aslan v Murphy [1990] 1 AC 417 ....148, 153
Austerberry v Corporation of Oldham (1885) 29 Ch D 750 ....117, 118, 121

BP Properties v Buckler (1987) 55 P & CR 337...158, 163
Bank of Ireland Home Mortgages v Bell [2001] 2 All ER 920 ....91, 95
Bannister v Bannister [1948] 2 All ER 133...38, 48
Barca v Mears [2005] 2 FLR 1 ....91, 100
Barclays Bank v O'Brien [1994] 1 AC 180 ....129, 137
Barclays Bank plc v Zaroovabli [1997] Ch 321..129, 136
Barrett v Halifax Building Society (1996) 28 HLR 634 ....129, 134
Barry v Haseldine [1952] Ch 832 ....104, 113
Basham, Re [1986] 1 WLR 1498 ....60, 66, 68
Batchelor v Marlow [2001] EWCA Civ 1051 107
Baxter v Four Oaks Properties Ltd [1965] 1 Ch 816 126
Bedson v Bedson [1965] 2 QB 666 ....91, 94
Berkley v Poulett (1977) 241 EG 911...1, 13
Bernstein v Skyviews, see Lord Bernstein of Leigh v Skyviews—
Biggs v Hoddinott [1898] 2 Ch 307..129, 130
Billson v Residential Apartments Ltd [1992] 1 AC 494 ....148, 156
Binions v Evans [1972] Ch 359 ....71, 78
Boosey v Davis (1987) 55 P & CR 83 ....158, 160
Bradley v Carritt [1903] AC 253 ....129, 131
Bridges v Hawkesworth (1851) 21 LJ QB 75 ....1, 6
British Railways Board v Glass [1965] Ch 587 ....104, 116
Bruton v London & Quadrant Housing Trust [2000] 1 AC 406 ....148, 149
Buchanan-Wollaston's Conveyance, Re [1939] Ch 738 ....91, 93
Buckinghamshire County Council v Moran [1990] Ch 623....................158, 161
Bull v Bull [1955] 1 QB 234 ....91, 92
Burgess v Rawnsley [1975] Ch 429...81, 88
Burns v Burns [1984] Ch 371...38, 51

CIBC Mortgages plc v Pitt [1994] 1 AC 200 ....129, 138
Case of Mines (1567) 1 Plowd 310...1, 5
Central Estates (Belgravia) v Woolgar (No 2) [1972] 1 WLR 1048 ....148, 156
Chelsea Yacht & Boat Co Ltd v Pope [2001] 2 All ER 409 ....1, 14

Cheltenham and Gloucester Building Society v Krausz [1997]
1 All ER 21 143
Cheltenham and Gloucester Building Society v Norgan [1996]
1 WLR 343, CA 130, 142
Chhokar v Chhokar [1984] FLR 313 ....28, 34
Citro, Re [1991] Ch 142..91, 99
City of London Building Society v Flegg [1988] AC 54......................28, 31, 32, 101
Cityland & Property (Holding) Ltd v Dabrah [1968] Ch 166 ....129, 135
Clore v Theatrical Properties Ltd [1936] 3 All ER 483.....................................71, 77
Coombes v Smith [1986] 1 WLR 808 ....60, 67, 68
Copeland v Greenhalf [1952] Ch 488 ....103, 106, 108
Cox v Jones [2004] 2 FLR 1010..38, 56
Crabb v Arun District Council [1976] Ch 179..60, 62
Crest Nicholson Residential (South) Ltd v McAllister [2003]
1 All ER 46, [2004] 1 WLR 2409...123
Crow v Wood [1971] 1 QB 77...109
Cuckmere Brick Co Ltd v Mutual Finance Ltd [1971] Ch 949 ....130, 145

D'Eyncourt v Gregory (1866) LR 3 Eq 382 ....1, 12
Dennis, Re [1993] Ch 72 ....81, 89
Dennis v Macdonald [1982] Fam 63 ....91, 98
Diligent Finance Co v Alleyne (1972) 23 P & CR 346 ....23, 24
Dodsworth v Dodsworth (1973) 228 EG 1115 ....60, 69
Dolphin's Conveyance, Re [1970] Ch 654 126
Drake v Whipp [1996] 1 FLR 826 ....38, 55
Draper's Conveyance, Re [1969] 1 Ch 81, 83
Dyer v Dyer (1788) 2 Cox Eq Cas 92..37, 39

ER Ives Investment Ltd v High [1967] 2 QB 379 ....23, 26, 60, 69, 121
Elitestone v Morris [1997] 2 All ER 513 ....1, 13, 14
Ellenborough Park, Re [1956] Ch 131 ....103, 104
Elliston v Reacher [1908] 2 Ch 374 ....117, 125, 126
Elwes v Brigg Gas Company (1886) 33 Ch D 562 ....1, 10
Errington v Errington & Woods [1952] 1 KB 290.................................71, 77, 78
Evers Trust, Re [1980] 1 WLR 1327 ....91, 94
Eves v Eves [1975] 1 WLR 1338 ....38, 49, 96

Fairclough v Swan Brewery Co [1912] AC 565 ....129, 133
Federated Homes Ltd v Mill Lodge Properties Ltd [1980]
1 WLR 594...117, 124, 126
First National Bank v Syed [1991] 2 All ER 250 144
First National Securities Ltd v Hegerty [1985] QB 850 ....81, 87
First Post Homes Ltd v Johnson [1995] 1 WLR 1567 ....17, 18
Four-Maids Ltd v Dudley Marshall [1957] Ch 317 140

Gascoigne v Gascoigne [1918] 1 KB 223 ....37, 44
Gillett v Holt [2001] Ch 210, [1998] 3 All ER 917 ....17, 20, 60, 64
Gissing v Gissing [1971] AC 886 ....37, 38, 40, 48, 54
Goldberg v Edwards [1950] Ch 247 ....103, 111
Goodman v Gallant [1986] 1 All ER 311...81, 82
Gore and Snell v Carpenter (1990) 60 P & CR 456....................................81, 86, 89
Grant v Edwards [1986] Ch 638 ....38, 50
Greasley v Cooke [1980] 1 WLR 1306...60, 65, 69, 71, 76
Greatorex v Newman [2008] EWCA Civ 1318 ....103, 108
Grigsby v Melville [1974] 1 WLR 80 ....1, 5

Halsall v Brizell [1957] Ch 169 ....70, 117, 121
Hamp v Bygrave (1983) 266 EG 720 ....1, 12

Harris v Goddard [1983] 1 WLR 1203 ....81, 84
Hibbert v McKiernan [1948] 2 KB 142 7
Hill v Tupper (1863) 2 H & C 121 ....103, 105
Hodgson v Marks [1971] Ch 892...29, 30
Holland v Hodgson (1872) LR 7 CP 328 ....1, 11, 12, 14
Holliday (a bankrupt), *Re* [1981] Ch 405..91, 100
Hounslow LBC v Twickenham Garden Development Ltd [1971]
  Ch 233 ....71, 73
Hunter v Canary Wharf Ltd [1997] 2 All ER 426 ....1, 4
Hurst v Picture Theatres Ltd [1915] 1 KB 1 ....71, 72
Hypo-Mortgage Services v Robinson [1997] 2 FLR 71 ....28, 34

International Tea Stores v Hobbs [1903] 2 Ch 165 ....103, 111
Inwards v Baker [1965] 2 QB 29 ....60, 63, 71, 76

Jaggard v Sawyer [1995] 1 WLR 269 ....117, 128
James v Thomas [2007] EWCA Civ 1212 38
Jelbert v Davis [1968] 1 WLR 589 ....104, 115
Jennings v Rice [2003] 1 P & CR 8 ....20, 60, 68, 69
Jeune v Queens Cross Properties Ltd [1974] Ch 97 ....148, 156
John Trenberth v National Westminster Bank (1979)
  39 P & CR 104...1, 3
Jones v Callenger [1961] 1 QB 176 ....91, 93, 96
Jones v Morgan [2002] 1 EGLR 125 ....129, 132

K (Deceased), *Re* [1985] Ch 85 ....81, 89
Kelsen v Imperial Tobacco [1957] 2 QB 334 ....1, 2
Kinch v Bullard [1998] 4 All ER 650 ....81, 84
King v David Allen & Sons (Billposting) Ltd [1916] 2 AC 54 ....71, 76
Kingsnorth Finance v Tizard [1986] 1 WLR 783 ....23, 26
Knightsbridge Estates Trust Ltd v Byrne [1939] Ch 441 ....129, 133
Kreglinger v New Patagonia Meat & Cold Storage Co Ltd [1914]
  AC 25 ....129, 131

Lace v Chantler [1944] KB 368 ....148, 151
Laiqat v Majid [2005] EWHC 1305 (QB) 1, 4
Lambeth LBC v Blackburn (2001) 82 P & CR 39 ....158, 163
Laskar v Laskar [2008] 1 WLR 2695 ....37, 41
Le Foe v Le Foe [2001] 2 FLR 970...38, 53
Leigh v Dickeson (1884) 15 QBD 60...91, 97
Lloyds Bank v Bundy [1975] QB 326...136
Lloyds Bank v Rosset [1991] 1 AC 107, HL *reversing* [1989]
  Ch 350 ....28, 32, 38, 52, 56
Lohia v Lohia [2001] WTLR 101 42
London & Blenheim Estates Ltd v Ladbroke Retail Parks Ltd [1992]
  1 WLR 1278..103, 107, 108
London County Council v Allen [1914] 3 KB 642........................117, 122
Lord Bernstein of Leigh v Skyviews & General Ltd [1978] QB 479.....1, 2
Lysaght v Edwards (1876) 2 Ch D 499 ....17, 22
Lyus v Prowsa Developments [1982] 1 WLR 1044 ....28, 36

McCausland v Duncan Lawrie [1997] 1 WLR 38 ....17, 19
McGrath v Wallace [1995] 2 FLR 114 ....37, 43
Malayan Credit Ltd v Jack Chia-MPH Ltd [1986] AC 549 (PC).......81, 82
Mancetter Development Ltd v Garmanson Ltd [1986] QB 1212..........1, 16
Matharu v Matharu (1994) 68 P & CR 93...62
Medforth v Blake [1999] 3 All ER 97...130, 146
Midland Bank plc v Cooke [1995] 4 All ER 562 ....38, 54

Midland Bank plc v Green [1891] AC 513...23, 24
Mills v Silver [1991] Ch 271 ....104, 114
Moffatt v Kazana [1969] 2 QB 152..1, 10
Moncrieff v Jamieson and others [2007] 1 WLR 2620 ....103, 108
Moody v Steggles (1879) 12 Ch D 261 ....103, 105
Mortgage Corporation v Shaire [2001] Ch 743 ....91, 94–96
Multiservice Bookbinding Ltd v Marden [1979] Ch 84 ....129, 134

National Provincial Bank v Ainsworth [1965] AC 1175................................28, 29, 78
National Westminster Bank v Morgan [1985] AC 686..136
Nicholls v Lan [2007] 1 FLR 744...91, 101

Oak Co-operative Building Society v Blackburn [1968] Ch 730 ....23, 24
Ofulue v Bossert [2009] 2 WLR 749, HL, Reversing in part [2008]
    3 WLR 1253, CA 158, 165
Oxley v Hiscock [2004] EWCA Civ 546 ....38, 56

P & A Swift Investments v Combined English Stores Group [1989]
    AC 632 ....117, 119
Paddington Building Society v Mendelsohn (1985)
    50 P & CR 244..28, 35
Palk v Mortgage Services Funding plc [1993] Ch 330 ....130, 141, 147
Paragon Finance plc v DB Thakerar & Co [1999] 1 All ER 400 ....37, 47
Paragon Finance plc v Nash [2002] 1 WLR 685 ....129, 135
Parker v British Airways Board [1982] QB 1004 ....1, 6, 9
Pascoe v Turner [1979] 1 WLR 431...60, 64, 68, 69
Peffer v Rigg [1977] 1 WLR 285 ....25, 28, 34
Pettit v Pettit [1970] AC 777 ....37, 39, 44
Pitt v Asset Management [1994] 1 WLR 327 ....17, 18
Powell v Macfarlane (1977) 38 P & CR 452 ....158, 160
Priors Case (1368) YB 42 Edw III 120
Prudential Assurance Co Ltd v London Residuary Body [1992]
    2 AC 386 ....148, 151
Pye (JA) (Oxford) Ltd v Graham [2001] Ch 804; [2002]
    3 All ER 865 ....158, 162
Pye (JA) (Oxford) Ltd v UK [2008] 46 EHRR 1083 ....158, 165, 166

Quennell v Maltby [1979] 1 All ER 568 ....130, 141

RB Policies at Lloyd's v Butler [1950] 1 KB 76 159
Rainbow Estates Ltd v Tokenhold [1999] Ch 64 ....148, 156
Ramsden v Dyson (1866) LR 1 HL 129...60, 61
Red House Farms (Thorndon) Ltd v Catchpole [1977]
    2 EGLR 125 ....158, 159
Rhone v Stephens [1994] 2 AC 310 ....117, 120
Roake v Chadha [1984] 1 WLR 40 ....117, 119
Rochefoucauld v Boustead [1897] 1 Ch 196...48
Rodway v Landy [2001] Ch 703..91, 96
Rogers v Hosegood [1900] 2 Ch 388 125
Royal Bank Of Scotland Ltd v Etridge (No 2) [1998]
    4 All ER 705 ....129, 138

Sharpe, Re [1980] 1 WLR 219 ....46, 71, 79
Skipton Building Society v Stott [2000] 2 All ER 779 146
Sledmore v Dalby (1996) 72 P & CR 196...60, 66
Smith & Snipes Hall Farm Ltd v River Douglas Catchment Board
    [1949] 2 KB 500..117, 118, 120

Somma v Hazelhurst [1978] 1 WLR 1014 ....148, 153
South Staffordshire Water Company v Sharman [1896] 2 QB 44 ....1, 8
Spectrum Investment Co v Holmes [1981] 1 WLR 221 164
Spiro v Glencrown Properties Ltd [1991] Ch 537 ....17, 19
Spyer v Phillipson [1931] 2 Ch 183 ....1, 15
St Marylebone Property Co Ltd v Fairweather [1963] AC 510......................158, 164
Stack v Dowden [2007] 2 AC 432 ....38, 46, 57, 81, 82
Stafford v Lee (1993) 65 P & CR 172 ....104, 113
Strand Securities v Caswell [1965] Ch 373 35
Street v Mountford [1985] AC 809 ....148, 150, 152, 153

TSB Bank plc v Botham [1996] EGCS 149 ....1, 15
Tanner v Tanner [1975] 1 WLR 1346 ....71, 75
Target Homes v Clothier [1994] 1 All ER 439...130, 144
Taylor v Dickens [1998] 3 FCR 455 ....17, 20, 60, 64
Taylor Fashions Ltd v Liverpool Trustees Co Ltd [1982]
    1 QB 133 ....60, 61
Tecbuild v Chamberlain (1969) 20 P & CR 633 ....158, 159
Thamesmead Town v Allotey (2000) 79 P & CR 557 121
Thomas v Sorrell (1673) Vaughan 330...71, 72
Thorner v Major [2009] UKHL 18 ....60, 65
Tinker v Tinker [1970] P 136 ....37, 45
Tinsley v Milligan [1994] 1 AC 340...37, 41, 44
Tribe v Tribe [1995] 4 All ER 236 ....37, 45
Tulk v Moxhay (1848) 2 Ph 744 ....117, 122

Union Lighterage Company v London Graving Dock Company
    [1902] 2 Ch 557 ....104, 115

Verrall v Great Yarmouth BC [1981] QB 202 ....71, 75
Virdi v Chana and another [2008] EWHC 2901 (Ch) 103, 109

Wakeham v Wood (1982) 43 P & CR 40 ....117, 127
Warren v Gurney [1944] 2 All ER 472...37, 43
Waverley Borough Council v Fletcher [1995] 3 WLR 772......................................1, 9
Westminster City Council v Clarke [1992] 2 AC 288 154
Wheeldon v Burrows (1879) 12 Ch D 31 ....103, 110, 111
Wheeler v JJ Saunders [1995] 2 All ER 697 ....104, 110
Williams v Hensman (1861) 1 John & H 546,
    30 LJ Ch 878 87
Williams v Staite [1979] Ch 291 ....60, 70
Williams & Glyn's Bank v Boland [1981] AC 487 ....23, 27, 29, 31, 32, 102
Willmott v Barber (1880) 15 Ch D 96...61, 62
Winter Garden Theatre (London) Ltd v
    Millennium Productions Ltd [1946] 1 All ER 678 ....71, 74
Wong v Beaumont Property Trust Ltd [1965] 1 QB 173............................103, 112
Wood v Leadbitter (1845) 13 M & W 838 ....71, 73
Wright v Macadam [1949] 2 KB 744...103, 107, 108, 112
Wrotham Park Estate Co Ltd v Parkside Homes Ltd [1974]
    1 WLR 798 ....117, 127, 128

Yaxley v Gotts [2000] 1 Ch 162 ....17, 20, 22
Yeoman's Row Management v Cobbe [2008] 1 WLR 1752.......................17, 21, 60
Young v Dalgety plc [1987] 1 EGLR 116..16

PREFACE

The Key Cases series is designed to give a clear understanding of important cases. This is useful when studying a new topic and invaluable as a revision aid.

Each case is broken down into fact and law. In addition, many cases are extended by the use of important extracts from the judgment or by comment or by highlighting problems. In some instances students are reminded that there is a link to other cases or material. If the link case is in another part of the same Key Cases book, the reference will be clearly shown. Some links will be to additional cases or materials that do not feature in the book.

To give a clear layout, symbols have been used at the start of each component of the case. The symbols are:

 Key Facts – These are the basic facts of the case.

 Key Law – This is the major principle of law in the case, the *ratio decidendi*.

 Key Judgment – This is an actual extract from a judgment made on the case.

 Key Comment – Influential or appropriate comments made on the case.

 Key Problem – Apparent inconsistencies or difficulties in the law.

 Key Link – This indicates other cases in the text which should be considered with this case.

At the start of each chapter there are mind maps highlighting the main cases and points of law. In addition, within most chapters, one or two of the most important cases are boxed to identify them and stress their importance.

Each Key Case book can be used in conjunction with the Key Facts book on the same subject. Equally, they can be used as additional material to support any other textbook.

This Key Case book on land law starts with an analysis of what we understand by land. It then considers different rights that exist in land, both formal and informal in law and in equity. The law is stated as I believe it to be on 1st June 2009.

Judith Bray

CHAPTER 1

THE DEFINITION OF 'LAND'

OWNERSHIP OF AIRSPACE ABOVE THE LAND
Kelsen v Imperial Tobacco (1957)
The landowner has as much of the airspace as is necessary for reasonable enjoyment of the land
Bernstein v Skyviews (1978)
No claim in trespass against someone taking aerial photographs of his home
John Trenberth v NatWest Bank (1979)
No common law right to enter land of another to facilitate repairs on own land
Hunter v Canary Wharf (1997)
The rights of a landowner do not extend to the protection of television reception
Laiqat v Majid (2005)
Even a very small interference with a landowner's airspace could constitute a trespass

Land

OWNERSHIP OF THE LAND FIXTURES AND FITTINGS
Holland v Hodgson (1872)
Fixtures are articles attached to the land and treated as part of the land
D'Eyncourt v Gregory (1866)
If the purpose of annexation is to enhance the land an item is a fixture
Hamp v Bygrave (1983)
If the purpose of annexation is to enhance the item it will be a chattel even if it is attached to the land
Berkley v Poulett (1977)
Heavy statues and a sundial remained chattels where there was evidence that they were frequently moved about the property
Elitestone v Morris (1997)
The main test to apply was purpose of annexation and not mode of annexation
Chelsea Yacht & Boat Co v Pope (2001)
Connection of essential services did not prevent a houseboat remaining a chattel
TSB Bank v Botham (1996)
Only domestic items with a high degree of annexation remain fixtures

TENANT'S FIXTURES
Spyer v Phillipson (1931)
A tenant cannot remove fixtures unless they come within trade; ornamental or agricultural fixtures
Mancetter Development Ltd v Garmanson Ltd (1986)
A tenant must make good any damage when removing tenant's fixtures.

OWNERSHIP BELOW THE SURFACE OF THE LAND
Case of Mines (1567)
The Crown has prerogative rights over gold and silver under the ground
Grigsby v Melville (1974)
The landowner owns the land immediately below the land

OWNERSHIP ITEMS FOUND ON THE LAND
Armory v Delamirie (1722)
A person who finds a chattel has a good claim against anyone except the true owner
Bridges v Hawkesworth (1851)
A claimant could keep unclaimed money found on the floor of a shop
Parker v British Airways Board (1982)
An occupier has a better right to chattels found on his land if he has manifested control over the building and anything found on it

OWNERSHIP OF ITEMS FOUND IN THE LAND
South Staffs Water Co v Sharman (1896)
Valuable rings found embedded in mud in a lake belonged to the landowner
Elwes v Brigg Gas Company (1886)
An item found buried in the land belonged to the true owner rather than the leaseholder
Moffatt v Kazana (1969)
Money hidden in a house belonged to a landowner or his estate even after he had moved from the house and later died
Waverley Borough Council v Fletcher (1995)
The occupier has a better claim to property if a finder is trespassing on the land

1.1 The definition of 'land'

1.1.1 Ownership of the airspace above the land

 HC *Kelsen v Imperial Tobacco* [1957] 2 QB 334

The claimant successfully claimed an injunction against the defendants based on trespass. They had hung an advertising sign which projected into the airspace above the claimant's land by four inches. Since it was an action in trespass an injunction could be granted without proof of any actual damage.

The landowner owns as much of the airspace as is necessary for his/her reasonable enjoyment of the land.

> **HC** *Lord Bernstein of Leigh v Skyviews & General Ltd* [1978] QB 479
>
> The defendants flew a light aircraft over the claimant's land, taking aerial photographs of his house. The claimant sued in trespass, arguing that he owned the airspace above his property. However it was held that no actionable trespass had occurred because the ownership of airspace was restricted to what was necessary for the landowner's reasonable enjoyment of property.
>
> The landowner's rights do not extend to rights in the airspace to an unlimited height.
>
> **Griffiths J**
> 'The problem is to balance the rights of an owner to enjoy the use of his land against the rights of the general public to take advantage of all that science

> now offers in the use of air space. This balance is in
> my judgment best struck in our present society by
> restricting the rights of an owner in the air space
> above his land to such height as is necessary for the
> ordinary use and enjoyment of his land and the
> structures upon it, and declaring that above that
> height he has no greater rights than any other
> member of the public.'

HC *John Trenberth Ltd v National Westminster Bank*
(1979) 39 P & CR 104

An injunction was sought by the claimants after the defendants
had erected scaffolding on their property without first gaining
their permission. The defendants had a statutory duty to repair
their property and this could only be carried out if scaffolding
was erected on the claimant's land. Permission to erect the
scaffolding had been persistently and irrationally refused.

The injunction was granted by the court. They declared that
the landowner has no specific right to enter the land of
another to carry out repairs.

The law has now been changed by the Access to Neighbouring
Land Act 1992 which allows landowners the right to go to
court to seek an order allowing them the right to enter the
land of another specifically to carry out essential repairs.

HC *Laiqat v Majid* **[2005] EWHC 1305 (QB)**

An extractor fan which projected over the claimant's land by 750 millimetres at a height of 4.5 metres constituted a trespass.

Even a very small interference with a landowner's airspace could constitute a trespass.

HL *Hunter v Canary Wharf Ltd* **[1997] 2 All ER 426**

Owners of properties in London unsuccessfully brought an action in nuisance against the owners of a tower block, arguing that it had interfered with television reception.

A landowner has rights in land which allow reasonable enjoyment and did not extend to rights to television reception.

This case also considered the rights of persons other than the landowner to bring an action in nuisance. It was held that such an action is confined to those who are linked to the land by some form of possessory claim and this did not extend to licensees.

1.2 Ownership below the surface of land

Case of Mines (1567) 1 Plowd 310

A challenge was made by the defendant, the Earl of Northumberland, that the Crown did not have the right to all gold and silver and precious metal found on a landowner's property.

It was held that gold and silver mines automatically belonged to the Crown as a prerogative right.

CA ***Grigsby v Melville*** [1974] 1 WLR 80

A cellar underneath the claimant's land could only be accessed from a neighbouring property but nevertheless the court held that it was owned by the claimant and the defendant his neighbour had to pay rent if he wanted to use it for storage.

The landowner owns the land immediately below his land even if it cannot be accessed easily from his land.

1.3 Items found in and on the land

1.3.1 Items found on the surface of the land

CA ***Armory v Delamirie*** (1722) 1 Strange 505 (93 ER 664)

A chimney sweep's boy found a ring. He took it to a jeweller who removed the stone and replaced it with glass and then refused to give it back to the boy. The court held that the jeweller must return the ring to the boy and replace the valuable jewel that had been removed.

The claimant who finds a chattel which has been lost has a good claim as against anyone, except the true owner.

HC *Bridges v Hawkesworth* (1851) 21 LJ QB 75

The claimant went to the defendant's shop on business and as he was leaving he found a small parcel lying on the floor of the shop. He found it contained a large sum of money.

He was able to claim the money for himself, based on the maxim 'finders keepers'.

CA   *Parker v British Airways Board* [1982] QB 1004

The claimant found a gold bracelet in the executive lounge at Heathrow airport. He handed it to the defendants for safekeeping while they sought the owner but he claimed it for himself if the true owner could not be found. It was held that the claimant was entitled to the bracelet. Although the British Airways Board had exercised a degree of control over the airport lounge this was limited to supervising admittance to the lounge. Proper control would include a lost property policy which was published to the passengers using the lounge.

Rights and liabilities of the occupier

1 An occupier of the land has rights superior to those of a finder over chattels in or attached to land.

2 An occupier of a building has rights superior to those of a finder over chattels upon or in, but not attached to, that building if, but only if, before the chattel is found, he has manifested an intention to exercise control over the building and the things which may be upon it or in it.

3 An occupier (within 2) is under an obligation to take such measures as in all the circumstances are reasonable to ensure that lost chattels are found and, upon their being found, whether by him or by a third party, to acquaint the true owner of the finding and to care for the chattels meanwhile.

Donaldson LJ

'On the evidence available there was no sufficient manifestation of any intention to exercise control over lost property before it was found, such as would give the defendants a right superior to that of the plaintiff or indeed any right over the bracelet. As the true owner has never come forward, it is a case of "finders keepers".'

 Hibbert v McKiernan [1948] 2 KB 142

In a criminal case the accused was charged with taking golf balls lost by players from a golf course with the intention of stealing them. It was maintained that the golf balls could not be stolen unless they were the property of the golf club.

The judge held that the defendant had no rights to the property since the golf balls were the property of the golf club.

Lord Goddard CJ
'Every householder or occupier of land means, or intends to exclude, thieves and wrongdoers from the property occupied by him, and this confers on him a special property in goods found on his land sufficient to support an indictment if the goods are taken therefrom, not under a claim of right, but with a felonious intent.'

CA *South Staffordshire Water Company v Sharman* [1896] 2 QB 44

Employees of the claimants found several valuable rings lodged in muddy water, while cleaning a pond.

It was held that they could not claim these for themselves because they were embedded in the land and therefore belonged to the landowner. They were not lying on the land.

Lord Russell CJ
'Where a person has possession of a house or land, with a manifest intention to exercise control over it and the things which may be upon it or in it, then, if something is found on that land, whether by an employee of the owner or by a stranger, the presumption is that the possession of that thing is in the owner of the *locus in quo*.'

1.3.2 Items found buried in the land

 CA *Parker v British Airways Board* [1982] QB 1004 (above)

Donaldson LJ
'The chattel is to be treated as an integral part of the realty as against all but the true owner, and so, incapable of being lost or that the finder has to do something to the realty in order to detach the chattel and, if he is not thereby to become a trespasser, will have to justify his actions by reference to some form of licence from the occupier. In all likely circumstances that licence will give the occupier a superior right to that of the finder.'

CA *Waverley Borough Council v Fletcher* [1995] 3 WLR 772

 The defendant used a metal detector in a public park and found a medieval brooch buried nine inches below the surface. He was allowed to use the metal detector in the park but he became a trespasser when he started digging in the land.

 It was held that the rights of the local authority landowner were superior to the rights of the claimant. The finder cannot claim his rights are superior to those of the landowner.

 The case of *Waverley* also looked at situations where an item may have worked its way just under the surface. In these cases the law may not consider the chattel as being attached to the land and the finder may have a good claim if the true owner does not come forward. What would the position be if a valuable piece of jewellery had fallen to the ground and rain, mud and leaves had later covered it? Would that now be part of the land?

Elwes v Brigg Gas Company (1886) 33 Ch D 562

A tenant found a prehistoric longboat whilst excavating the leased land. He claimed it for himself as occupier of the land but was unsuccessful. The item was buried in the land and clearly had been in the land when the tenant had entered the land.

The rights of the freeholder were held to be superior to the rights of the leaseholder because the item had become buried long before the lease had been granted.

1.3.3 The true owner

 Moffatt v Kazana [1969] 2 QB 152

The defendant found money hidden in a biscuit tin in the roof of his house three years after he had bought it. It was proved that the money had belonged to the vendor who had forgotten all about it. He had died and the land was sold to the defendant.

It was held that the deceased's estate had a good claim to the money because the true owner has a better claim over property than the finder or the landowner in whose land the items are found, unless he has abandoned the items.

Wrangham J
'If Mr Russell never got rid of the notes, that is to say, never got rid of ownership of the notes, he continued to be the owner of them and, if he continued to be the owner of them, he had title to those notes which nobody else, whether the owner of the land in which they were found, or the finders, or anybody else would have.'

1.4 Fixtures and fittings

1.4.1 The test for fixtures

HC *Holland v Hodgson* (1872) LR 7 CP 328

A number of spinning looms were nailed to the floor of a factory and the mortgagee claimed ownership of the looms when he took possession of the premises. The court held they were fixtures and were therefore part of the land.

Articles attached to the land only by their own weight are not part of the land unless it can be shown that that was intended. However, articles attached to the land, even if the degree of attachment is slight, are to be considered part of the land, and therefore fixtures, unless circumstances suggest that they were intended to continue to be a chattel.

The tests therefore relate to:

i) the degree or mode of annexation;
ii) the general purpose of annexation.

Blackburn J
'Thus blocks of stone placed one on top of another without any mortar or cement for the purpose of forming a dry stone wall would become part of the land though the same stones if deposited in a builder's yard and for convenience sake stacked on the top of each other in the form of a wall would remain chattels.'

CA *D'Eyncourt v Gregory* (1866) LR 3 Eq 382

Several stone figures and statues passed as fixtures although they were attached by their own weight and could be easily removed from the land because they were part of the overall architectural design.

Where the purpose of annexation was to enhance the land rather than to enhance the chattel, an item would be held to be a fixture.

HC *Hamp v Bygrave* (1983) 266 EG 720

A number of stone urns, stone ornaments and statues standing on their own weight were claimed as chattels by the vendors. A single stone plinth was affixed to the ground. They also claimed patio lights fixed to the wall.

In applying the two tests from *Holland v Hodgson* (above) for chattels the court held that items firmly fixed to the land could remain chattels if the purpose of annexation was to enjoy them as chattels and the degree of annexation was necessary for the items themselves. In applying this test they were all held to be chattels.

CA | *Berkley v Poulett* (1977) 241 EG 911

The purchaser of land claimed that a sundial, some statues and a number of pictures fixed into recesses in a panelled room removed by the vendor on sale were fixtures and should be returned. It was held that since they did not constitute part of a grand architectural design they could not pass as fixtures. There was evidence that the owners often moved the statues and the sundial about the garden. This suggested that they remained chattels. However, a plinth on which the items sometimes rested remained a fixture.

Scarman LJ

'A degree of annexation which in earlier times the law would have treated as conclusive may now prove nothing. If the purpose of the annexation be for the better enjoyment of the object itself, it may remain a chattel, notwithstanding a high degree of physical annexation. Clearly, however, it remains significant to discover the extent of physical disturbance of the building or the land involved in the removal of the object. If an object cannot be removed without serious damage to, or destruction of, some part of the realty, the case for its having become a fixture is a strong one.'

HL | *Elitestone v Morris* [1997] 2 All ER 513

A number of chalet homes had been built near Swansea. They rested on concrete pillars which were attached to the ground. Although similar to mobile homes, they could not be moved without demolition. The claimant had been served with a notice to quit by the owner of the land but claimed that he had protection under the Rent Acts. He could only claim this if the chalet bungalow was part of the realty and not a chattel. The court held that the house was a fixture and formed part of the realty.

The main test to apply was the purpose of annexation and not the degree of annexation. Even if a structure could be removed it might still be a fixture. However, where a structure cannot be removed without demolition then it must be a fixture.

 Chelsea Yacht and Boat Co Ltd v Pope [2001] 2 All ER 409

A houseboat was permanently moored and essential services had been connected. It was claimed that because of this the houseboat had become part of the land and would pass as a fixture.

It was held that as the boat could easily be moved to another stretch of water, without incurring damage to the boat, it remained a chattel. The essential services could be easily disconnected from the boat.

The difficulty here is that some items start life as chattels but are then used in such a way that they will become part of the property and therefore are fixtures. If a pile of stones is waiting to be made into a path then the stones have not yet become fixtures and remain chattels until the building work has been done. This point was illustrated by Blackburn J in *Holland v Hodgson* and later considered in *Elitestone v Morris*.

Issues concerning ownership of chattels are usually decided between the parties and by reference to the Standard Conditions of Sale which are in general use in conveyancing.

1.4.2 Everyday objects

TSB Bank plc v Botham [1996] EGCS 149

The bank repossessed and sold a flat that had been owned by Mr Botham. He claimed that a number of everyday items were chattels and remained his property.

It was held that items with a high degree of annexation, such as kitchen worksurfaces, bathroom fittings and the kitchen units, were all fixtures. Items deemed to be white goods, such as the cooker, fridge, freezer and washing machine, were all chattels. Items attached in an insubstantial way, such as curtains, carpets and blinds and light fittings, were all chattels.

Roch LJ

Roch LJ considered why bathroom fittings were fixtures: 'They are not there … to be enjoyed for themselves, but they are there as accessories which enable the room to be used and enjoyed as a bathroom. Viewed objectively, they were intended to be permanent and to afford a lasting improvement to the property.'

1.4.3 Tenant's fixtures

Spyer v Phillipson [1931] 2 Ch 183

A tenant had installed antique panelling. This was considered to be ornamental and therefore the tenant could remove this so long as it did not damage the property.

A tenant cannot remove fixtures unless they come within one of three categories: trade fixtures, agricultural fixtures or domestic or ornamental fixtures.

CA ***Young v Dalgety plc*** [1987] 1 EGLR 116

Light fittings and a carpet installed by a tenant could be removed because they were trade fixtures.

CA ***Mancetter Developments Ltd v Garmanson Ltd***
[1986] QB 1212

Tenants who ran a chemical business claimed the right to remove an extractor fan from the wall of their premises.

The extractor fan could be removed so long as the tenant made good the damage to the property. In this case the extractor fan had left a large hole which had to be made good by the tenant.

Dillon LJ
'The analysis of the liability at common law is … that the liability to make good the damage is a condition of the tenant's right to remove tenant's fixtures: therefore removal of the fixtures without making good the damage, being in excess of the tenant's right of removal, is waste, actionable in tort, just as much as removal by the tenant of a landlord's fixture which the tenant has no right to remove is waste.'

CHAPTER 2

TRANSFER AND CREATION OF RIGHTS IN LAND

RIGHTS PRIOR TO EXCHANGE OF CONTRACTS

Pitt v Asset Management (1994)

A lock-out agreement will give the purchaser rights to recover damages for breach of agreement but it does not give rights to enforce a sale against the vendor

First Post Homes v Johnson (1995)

Contracts for the sale or disposition of an interest in land must be in writing and incorporate all terms and be signed by both parties

Spiro v Glencrown Properties Ltd (1991)

The exercise of an option to purchase land does not have to comply with s 2 LP(MP)A 1989

McCausland v Duncan Lawrie (1997)

An informal variation of terms of a contract had to comply with s 2 LP(MP)A 1989 in order to be enforceable

---

↕

AVOIDANCE OF THE STRICT FORMALITIES OF TRANSFER

Yaxley v Gotts (2000)

No writing is required where rights in land are acquired under a constructive trust or proprietary estoppel

See also: *Taylor v Dickens* (1998)

Gillett v Holt (2001)

Yeoman's Row Management v Cobbe Ltd (2008)

↕

EFFECT IN LAW OF EXCHANGE OF CONTRACTS

Lysaght v Edwards (1876)

Once there is a valid exchange of contracts for sale the vendor becomes a trustee for the purchaser of the estate sold

2.1 Rights prior to exchange of contracts

 Pitt v Asset Management [1994] 1 WLR 327

A lock-out agreement between the vendor and the purchaser, specifying that the vendor would not accept any offers for a specified period, was held to be enforceable between the parties.

The purchaser will not have any enforceable rights in land until contracts are exchanged between the parties. This leaves a purchaser vulnerable to the possibility of being 'gazumped' by another purchaser offering more money to the vendor. 'Gazumping' can be restricted if the purchaser enters into a lock-out agreement with the vendor. A lock-out agreement is a prior collateral contract for consideration that during a stipulated period the vendor will not negotiate with anyone else. It does not give the purchaser the right to enforce sale but entitles the purchaser to recover damages for breach of the agreement.

 First Post Homes Ltd v Johnson [1995] 1 WLR 1567

The purchaser had prepared a letter for the vendor to sign: the purchaser's name was typed at the top of the letter. The purchaser had signed the plan mentioned in the letter but not the letter itself. There was no contract because the plan did not refer to the letter and the purchaser had not signed the contract as required by statute.

Under s 2 the Law of Property (Miscellaneous Provisions) Act (LP(MP)A) 1989 contracts for the sale or disposition of an interest in land must be in writing, incorporate all terms and be signed by both parties.

HC *Spiro v Glencrown Properties Ltd* [1991] Ch 537

A notice to exercise an option had only been signed by one of the parties. It was held to be effective even though only one party had signed it. Although the initial grant of the option had to comply with s.2 the exercise of the option did not.

CA *McCausland v Duncan Lawrie* [1997] 1 WLR 38

In this case the completion date had been stipulated in the original enforceable contract. The parties informally rearranged the completion date for another day. The solicitors for the two parties exchanged letters varying the completion date. The court held that this was not an effective variation of contract because both parties had not signed the contract and it did not satisfy s 2. The first completion date remained enforceable.

If the parties to a contract informally vary the terms from those agreed in a formal contract it will not be an effective variation of contract satisfying s 2 of the LP(MP)A 1989 and will not be enforceable by the parties.

2.2 Avoidance of the strict formalities of transfer

 Yaxley v Gotts [2000] 1 Ch 162

The claimant was a self-employed builder who agreed to carry out works on a property already divided into flats and in return he was to acquire rights over the ground floor of the house by the first defendant. This arrangement was not put into writing. The second defendant purchased the property and after an argument the claimant was excluded from the property. In spite of the lack of written agreement the claimant was granted rights in the property.

The judges in the Court of Appeal did not agree on which basis the claimant's rights should be upheld. Robert Walker LJ favoured a constructive trust whereas Clarke and Beldam LJJ suggested that proprietary estoppel could be used where an agreement for the transfer of an interest in land had not been put into writing but they both agreed that a constructive trust was also appropriate.

Consider the nature of proprietary estoppel in **Chapter 6** and the issues arising in cases where promises have been made to leave someone property in a will: *Taylor v Dickens* [1998] 3 FCR 455; *Gillett v Holt* [2001] Ch 210; *Jennings v Rice* [2003] 1 P & CR 8.

Yeoman's Row Management v Cobbe [2008] 1 WLR 1752

The owner of a building and a developer reached an oral agreement in principle under which the developer would obtain planning permission to develop the property and the property would be transferred to him for development and later sale and distribution of the profits between the parties. The developer obtained the planning permission and sought to enforce the agreement even though it had never been put in writing. The House of Lords refused the developer's claim.

The House of Lords (reversing the Court of Appeal) held that the claimant was not entitled to a share in the increase in value of the property under the doctrine of proprietary estoppel. This was because the doctrine only applies where the claimant had an expectation of a certain interest in land. In this case both parties knew that the deal had not yet been completed and that the contract had to be in writing under s 2 LP(MP) Act 1989 and therefore there was no expectation of a certain interest in land.

The House of Lords also suggested that proprietary estoppel would be inappropriate for commercial transactions.

Scott LJ

'S 2 of the 1989 Act declares to be void any agreement for the acquisition of an interest in land that does not comply with the requisite formalities prescribed by the section. Subsection(5) expressly makes an exception for resulting, implied or constructive trusts. They may validly come into existence without compliance with the prescribed formalities.

Proprietary estoppel does not have the benefit of this exception … proprietary estoppel cannot be prayed in aid in order to render enforceable an agreement that statute has declared to be void.'

The House of Lords appear to be suggesting that a constructive trust may be used to uphold an oral contract for the sale of land but the case of *Yaxley v Gotts* was not discussed in the speeches.

2.3 The effect in law of exchange of contracts

 Lysaght v Edwards (1876) 2 Ch D 499

The Master of the Rolls, Jessel MR, held that once there is a valid contract for sale the vendor holds the estate on trust for the purchaser.

CHAPTER 3

UNREGISTERED LAND

Midland Bank v Green (1981)
An unregistered land charge will not be binding under the Land Charges Act 1972 even where the purchaser buys with actual notice

↑

KEY ISSUES IN UNREGISTERED CONVEYANCING

Kingsnorth Finance v Tizard (1986)
A purchaser will be fixed with notice of an interest in property unless proper inquiries are made
KEY LINK
Williams & Glyn's Bank v Boland (1981) (registered land)

↓

Diligent Finance Co Ltd v Alleyne (1972)
Oak Co-operative Building Society v Blackburn (1968)

↓

ER Ives Investment Ltd v High (1967)
Where a right is not registrable the doctrine of notice will apply

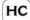 **Diligent Finance Co v Alleyne** (1972) 23 P & CR 346

The legal title to a house was owned by the husband and on the conveyance his name was Erskine Owen Alleyne. His wife registered a Class F land charge against the name Erskine Alleyne. He later granted a mortgage to a finance company who searched against the incorrect name. It was held that the incorrect registration did not affix the finance company with actual notice so that it took priority over the interest of the wife.

 Oak Co-operative Building Society v Blackburn [1968] Ch 730

The legal owner of some property was called Francis David Blackburn. An interest was registered against the name of Frank David Blackburn. The plaintiff argued that the registration was invalid. The court held that as an incorrect name had been used requisitioning the search, then the use of an incorrect name in the initial registration was not ineffective.

Russell LJ
'... if there be registration in what may be fairly described as a version of the full names of the vendor, albeit not a version which is bound to be discovered on a search in the correct full names, we would not hold it a nullity against someone who does not search at all, or (as here) searches in the wrong name..'

 Midland Bank v Green [1981] AC 513

The owner of land granted his son an option to purchase the

land for £22,500. This should have been registered as an estate contract as a class C(iv) land charge but the son failed to do so. After an argument with his son the father tried to revoke the option. When he discovered that the option had not been registered the father decided to convey the land, which had nearly doubled in value, to his wife with the sole purpose of defeating the rights of the son. It was sold for £500 which was a fraction of its proper value. The son later tried to exercise the option but it was declared void. It had been defeated on the sale to the wife.

It was held by unanimous decision in the House of Lords that the option was defeated by the sale from the father to the mother. The wife and children of the now deceased son could not claim the right to exercise the option to buy at the original price of £22,500. The true value had risen to over £109,000.

Under the land charges scheme in unregistered conveyancing, failure to register an interest in the land such as a restrictive covenant or an estate contract is fatal as against a purchaser for value. Issues of actual notice and bad faith are irrelevant.

There will be a sale where the purchaser has paid 'money or money's worth' and he or she has thereby provided valuable consideration. In this context valuable consideration includes nominal consideration so the very small sum paid by the mother to the husband was deemed to be consideration.

Peffer v Rigg [1977] 1 WLR 285 (see registered conveyancing in **Chapter 4**). In this case it was held that under the Land Registration Act 1925 a purchaser had to be in good faith to take advantage of the failure to protect a minor interest.

This case no longer applies since the introduction of the Land Registration Act 2002 which does not include any reference to acting in good faith and under s 29 Land Registration Act 2002 the concept of actual notice has not been reintroduced so an interest will not bind unless it is entered on the register or is itself overriding.

CA *ER Ives Investment Ltd v High* **[1967] 2 QB 379**

A right of way had been granted to the claimants, but it had not been completed by deed of grant and was not registered at the Land Charges Register as a Class D (iii) land charge as assumed would be necessary for it to take effect as a right in unregistered land.

It was successfully argued that the nature of the right was such that it fell outside the rules requiring registration and therefore the doctrine of notice would apply and it was held to be binding.

HC *Kingsnorth Finance v Tizard* **[1986] I WLR 783**

A husband held the legal title to the matrimonial home on implied trust for himself and his wife in equal shares; the title was unregistered. After the relationship broke down the wife moved out, leaving the husband and the two children living in the house. The wife frequently visited the house in order to carry out certain household chores. The husband took out a mortgage on the property, falsely representing that the property was his own and no one else had an interest. The husband arranged a visit from the agent of the mortgagees on a day when he knew his wife would not be there. The husband defaulted on the mortgage and the mortgagee sought possession of the property.

The court held that the mortgagees had failed to make proper enquiries and were fixed with notice of the wife's interest in the property. The court held that she had been in occupation when the agent visited since occupation did not have to be 'exclusive, continuous or uninterrupted'.

Consider the position in registered land. The rights of the wife in this case were not registrable, they were dependent on actual notice and the failure of the agent to check whether anyone had rights in the property. In registered land such rights are capable of entry on the register but they are also capable of binding a purchaser as an overriding interest if the claimant is in occupation.

Consider *Williams & Glyn's Bank v Boland* [1981] AC 487 (**Chapter 4**).

REGISTERED LAND

IMPLIED POSTPONEMENT
Paddington Building Society v Mendelsohn (1985)

PERSONAL RIGHTS CANNOT BIND THIRD PARTIES
National Provincial Bank v Ainsworth (1965)
At common law a spouse does not automatically acquire a proprietary right in land

NATURE OF OVERRIDING INTERESTS
Hodgson v Marks (1971)
Overriding rights bind a third party and do not require registration
Williams & Glyn's Bank v Boland (1981)
Equitable rights in land can be both registrable as a burden and be overriding
Lloyds Bank v Rosset (1989)
An overriding interest is based on proof of equitable rights and actual occupation and will fail if either is not present
City of London Building Society v Flegg (1988)
Equitable rights in land can be overreached where the purchase money is paid to two trustees in land

GOOD FAITH
Peffer v Rigg (1977)
A minor interest will still be binding if the purchaser does not buy in good faith
NOTE: Since the Land Registration Act 2002 it is not relevant whether a sale is in good faith or not

ACTUAL OCCUPATION
Lloyds Bank v Rosset (1989)
The presence of a builder can sometimes constitute actual occupation on behalf of a claimant
Abbey National v Cann (1991)
An overriding interest will only be binding if the claimant is in actual occupation at the date of disposition
Hypo-Mortgage Services v Robinson (1997)
Children cannot claim to be in actual occupation independent of their parents
Chhokar v Chhokar (1981)
A claimant is in actual occupation of land even where temporarily absent.

CONSTRUCTIVE TRUSTS
Lyus v Prowsa Developments (1982)
An unregistered right may be binding under a constructive trust if the purchaser buys expressly subject to the right

4.1 Personal rights cannot bind third parties and cannot be overriding

National Provincial Bank Ltd v Ainsworth [1965] AC 1175

A husband left his wife and she remained in the matrimonial home. The property was in the sole name of the husband and he transferred it to his company and later he took out a mortgage to the bank in the name of the company. The issue before the court was the exact nature of the wife's rights.

Although a deserted wife may have a personal right to occupy the former matrimonial home, it is not a right capable of binding a third party purchaser. It is not a proprietary right in land.

The key feature of registered land is the registration of title at the Land Registry. A number of important statutory rights can be protected by notice in the charges register of an individual title. These rights would include restrictive covenants and equitable easements. Today they also include matrimonial rights under the Family Law Act 1996 but such rights were not originally recognised under the Land Registration Act 1925.

Lord Wilberforce
'The wife's rights, as regards the occupation of her husband's property, are essentially of a personal kind: personal in the sense that a decision can only be reached on the basis of considerations essentially dependent on the mutual claims of husband and wife as spouses and as a result of a broad weighing of circumstances and merit.'

A number of statutes passed after this case, including the Matrimonial Homes Acts 1967 and 1983 and the Family Law Act 1996, all give effect to the rights of the spouse who does not own the property at law or in equity and allow such rights to be registered as a charge at the Land Registry. Such rights will only be binding if they are entered on the register.

4.2 Overriding rights

4.2.1 The nature of an overriding interest

CA *Hodgson v Marks* [1971] Ch 892

Mrs Hodgson took a lodger who persuaded her to transfer the title of the property to him. She remained in occupation of the property. The lodger later sold the property to Mr Marks and then almost immediately died. It was held that before his transfer to Marks the lodger held the property on trust for Mrs Hodgson and her rights were overriding and binding on the purchaser Mr Marks and subsequently on his estate.

In limited circumstances the law has held some rights in land to be both registrable and also overriding. Overriding interests are rights that bind the registered proprietor although they are not entered on the register.

Overriding interests were introduced under s 70(1) Land Registration Act 1925 and covered many rights, in particular the rights of anyone who had an interest in the land who was in actual occupation of the property. They continue to be recognised under Sched 1 and 3 of the LRA 2002.

HL *Williams & Glyn's Bank v Boland* [1981] AC 487

A husband was registered as sole legal owner of the matrimonial home. The wife had made contributions to the purchase and she should have registered her rights in equity as a minor interest. She failed to do so but the court found that her interest in the property was still protected as an overriding interest because she had both an equitable interest in the property and was in actual occupation. If there had been a second trustee her rights would have been overreached, thereby transferring them from the property into rights in the purchase monies.

HL *City of London Building Society v Flegg* [1988] AC 54

The title of property was registered in the name of a man and his wife, although part of the purchase price had been paid by the wife's parents. The legal title was held on trust by the son-in-law and daughter for themselves and the parents-in-law. The husband and wife took out a mortgage and then defaulted on the repayments and the building society repossessed the property.

It was found that although the parents-in-law had an interest in the land and were in actual occupation their interests were overreached. This was because the capital monies had been transferred to two trustees as required for overreaching to take effect.

Lord Oliver
'Once the beneficiary's rights have been shifted from the land to capital monies in the hands of the trustees, there is no longer an interest in the land to which the occupation can be referred or which it

can protect. If the trustees sell in accordance with the statutory provisions, so overreaching the beneficial interests in reference to the land, nothing remains to which a right of occupation can attach.'

Consider the difference that a second trustee can make to the rights of the equitable owner. How can you account for the different approach that the law takes in a case such as *Flegg* from a case like *Williams & Glyn's Bank v Boland*?

CA *Lloyds Bank v Rosset* [1989] Ch 350

A house in need of renovation was purchased in the sole name of the husband. The work was started prior to the completion and was shared between the builders and the wife.

The wife claimed an overriding interest in the house, based on her actual occupation and her equitable interest. She had difficulty in proving both requirements.

In the Court of Appeal the wife claimed she was in actual occupation before the transfer, which would give her rights priority over the mortgagees. She claimed that she had an equitable interest based on her contributions to the building work.

The court was prepared to find that she was in actual occupation, but on appeal to the House of Lords her claim for a beneficial interest failed so the issue of actual occupation was not further discussed.

Nicholls LJ

'In my view the presence of a builder engaged by a householder to do work for him in a house is to be regarded as the presence of the owner when considering whether or not the owner is in actual occupation.'

This case also considered whether the wife had a beneficial interest in the property. This is considered under constructive trusts in **Chapter 5**.

4.2.2 When does actual occupation begin?

 HL *Abbey National v Cann* [1991] 1 AC 56

The claimant was the mother of the legal owner of the property. She was away on holiday on the day of completion but her furniture arrived and the removal men started to move it into the house 35 minutes before completion.

The court found that she was not in actual occupation before completion and so her rights were not binding on the mortgagees who had provided part of the purchase monies to the claimant. A claim of an overriding interest based on actual occupation could only succeed where the claimant was already in actual occupation of the land at the disposition. Occupation must be obvious at the time of disposition.

.2.3 Have children a separate claim to an overriding right?

  Hypo-Mortgage Services v Robinson [1997] 2 FLR 71

Minor children cannot claim to be in actual occupation of property, independent of their parents, since they are only there as 'shadows of occupation' of their parent.

4.2.4 Temporary absences

  Chhokar v Chhokar [1984] FLR 313

A husband held the registered title of the matrimonial home on trust for himself and his wife in equal shares. He secretly agreed to transfer the title to a friend whilst his wife was in hospital having a baby, and all the locks were changed. The husband disappeared with the proceeds of sale and when the wife arrived home from hospital she found that she was denied access.

The court held that she had been in actual occupation in spite of her temporary absence from the property and so her rights were binding on the third party purchaser. The fact that her possessions remained in the property was symbolic of her occupation.

4.2.5 The issue of good faith

  Peffer v Rigg [1977] 1 WLR 285

Two brothers-in-law purchased a house for their mother-in-law. It was put into the name of one brother but both contributed equally. The owner sold the house to his estranged wife for £1 as part of a divorce settlement. He was aware that such a sale would defeat the claim of the other brother-in-law because he had failed to enter his interest on the register. He could not claim an overriding right because he was not in actual occupation of the property.

It was held by Graham J that a purchaser had to be in good faith to take advantage of the failure to protect a minor interest. The wife was not a purchaser in good faith because she knew that the sale to her would defeat her brother-in-law's interest in a house to which he had contributed half the sale price.

This depended on a provision in the Land Registration Act 1925 which has been left out of the Land Registration Act 2002. This means that good faith should play no part in issues regarding failure to register a right.

It was commented by Cross J in *Strand Securities v Caswell* [1965] Ch 373 that it was 'vital to the working of the land registration system that notice of something which is not on the register should not affect a transferee unless it is an overriding interest'.

An equitable interest cannot be binding as an interest that overrides unless the claimant is in actual occupation.

 Paddington Building Society v Mendelsohn (1985) 50 P & CR 244

Property was purchased partly by a son and his mother with the title registered in his name alone. The mother was fully aware that the purchase money was to be partly provided by a mortgage loan provided by a building society. The mother later claimed that her interest took priority to that of the building society since she had both an interest under a resulting trust and was in actual occupation of the property.

The occupier had impliedly consented to the creation of the mortgage. The acquisition of rights in favour of the mother was dependent on the mortgage which meant that the mother in occupation could not claim an interest, which had priority to the rights of the building society.

4.3 Unregistered rights in registered land existing as constructive trusts

HC *Lyus v Prowsa Developments Ltd* [1982] 1 WLR 1044

A purchaser of property promised to take the land subject to an unprotected interest. An estate contract had not been entered on the register prior to sale. The subsequent sale should therefore have defeated the interest.

The right was binding on the purchaser although it had not been registered because the purchase expressly took subject to the right. The court held that the vendor held the property subject to a constructive trust in favour of the claimant.

CHAPTER 5

EQUITABLE RIGHTS IN LAND: RESULTING AND CONSTRUCTIVE TRUSTS

RESULTING TRUSTS

PRESUMPTION OF A RESULTING TRUST

Dyer v Dyer (1788)
A trust of a legal estate will result to the person advancing the purchase money
Pettit v Pettit (1970); *Gissing v Gissing* (1971)
A resulting trust will arise if contributions are made to the purchase of property.
Improvements to property do not constitute contributions
Laskar v Laskar (2008)
The presumption of joint ownership would not apply if property was purchased as
an investment even if the owners were members of the same family. It was more
appropriate to find a resulting trust and to apportion shares according to the value
of each contribution.

PRESUMPTION OF ADVANCEMENT

Warren v Gurney (1944)
A presumption of a resulting trust is rebutted by a presumption of advancement
McGrath v Wallace (1995)
A presumption of advancement can be rebutted by contrary evidence
Tinsley v Milligan (1994)
A presumption of a resulting trust is not rebutted by an illegal motive if that
motive is not relied on as a basis for the resulting trust
Gascoigne v Gascoigne (1918); *Tinker v Tinker* (1970)
An illegal motive cannot be used to rebut the presumption of advancement
Tribe v Tribe (1995)
An illegal motive can be relied on to rebut the presumption of advancement if the
illegal purpose was not carried out

CONSTRUCTIVE TRUSTS

DEFINITION

Paragon Finance Plc v DB Thakerar & Co (1999)
A constructive trust arises by operation of law whenever the circumstances are
such that it would be unconscionable for the owner of property to assert
ownership and to deny the rights of others

Bannister v Bannister (1948)
An express trust under s 53(1)(b) LPA 1925 must be evidenced in writing but an implied trust under s 53(2) does not require written evidence
Gissing v Gissing (1971)
A constructive trust can arise where there is evidence of a common intention

EVIDENCE OF A COMMON INTENTION

Eves v Eves (1975); *Grant v Edwards* (1986)
Evidence of a common intention can either be express or implied
Burns v Burns (1984)
Without evidence of a common intention, contributions in kind will not support a constructive trust
Lloyds Bank v Rosset (1991)
Indirect contributions cannot support a constructive trust unless there is a common intention to share
Le Foe v Le Foe (2001)
A small direct contribution and contributions over a period of time towards household expenses could give rise to evidence of a common intention
James v Thomas (2007)
A constructive trust can arise some years after the property has been acquired by and registered in the sole name of one party but if there is no express agreement the court will be slow to infer an agreement

ASSESSING THE SHARE IN RESULTING and CONSTRUCTIVE TRUSTS

Midland Bank plc v Cooke (1995)
Evidence of shared finances throughout a marriage showed an intention to share property equally in spite of a 7% contribution to the purchase price
Drake v Whipp (1996)
A joint bank account and contributions to family expenses were evidence of an intention to share the family home
Cox v Jones (2004)
A supervisory role over building works holding back career progression could constitute detriment
Oxley v Hiscock (2004)
Quantification of shares in property under all implied trusts should be based on fairness rather than purely size of contributions
Stack v Dowden (2007)
Where the legal title is held jointly it is presumed that the equitable interest will be held jointly. This presumption can be rebutted by contrary evidence

5.1 Resulting trusts

5.1.1 The presumption of a resulting trust

Dyer v Dyer (1788) 2 Cox Eq Cas 92

Eyre CB
'A trust of a legal estate ... whether taken in the names of the purchasers and others jointly, or in the names of others without that of the purchaser; whether in one name or several; whether jointly or successive, results to the man who advances the purchase-money.'

HL *Pettitt v Pettitt* [1970] AC 777

A house was owned by a wife and on divorce her husband sought to claim a share, relying on his contributions in kind. He had redecorated the house and improved the property and he claimed that this had increased the value of the house.

Although the Court of Appeal found that he had a share, the House of Lords disagreed and only allowed him the cost of the improvements and not a proportionate share in the total value of the house equivalent to his improvements.

Lord Upjohn
'(W)here both spouses contribute to the acquisition of property, then my own view ... is that they intended to be joint beneficial owners and this is so whether the purchase be in the joint names or in the name of one. This is the result of an application of the presumption of resulting trust.'

HL *Gissing v Gissing* [1971] AC 886

On divorce, a wife claimed a share in the matrimonial home solely owned by her husband. Over the 30-year marriage she had made a number of contributions in kind, such as the purchase of furniture and household equipment and contributions towards improvements carried out in the house. The Court of Appeal found in her favour but the House of Lords held that she could not claim an equitable interest.

Lord Pearson reconsidered the issue of when a resulting trust will arise and suggested that the reason a resulting trust is presumed is because it gives effect to the intentions of the parties at the time when the contributions were made. However, the presumption is a rebuttable presumption and it can be rebutted by evidence showing some other intention.

Lord Diplock
'A resulting, implied or constructive trust – and it is unnecessary for the present purposes to distinguish between these three classes of trust – created by a transaction between the trustee and the beneficiary in connection with the acquisition by the trustee of a legal estate in land, whenever the trustee has so conducted himself that it would be inequitable to allow him to deny to the beneficiary a beneficial interest in the land acquired.'

This case also raised issues relating to constructive trusts and is reconsidered in detail below at **5.2**.

CA *Laskar v Laskar* [2008] 1 WLR 2695

A mother and daughter purchased property in joint names as an investment. The mother was solely responsible for the property and for the mortgage repayments. The relationship between the mother and her daughter broke down and the daughter sought an order declaring that she had a half share in the property.

Since the purchase of the property was nothing more than a business venture, the relationship was one between investors and the presumption of joint ownership did not apply in such circumstances even where the parties were members of the same family. This was a resulting trust and each party was entitled to the value of her own contribution.

HL *Tinsley v Milligan* [1994] 1 AC 340

Miss T and Miss M were lovers and together they jointly contributed to the purchase of property. The title was placed in T's name alone in order to allow M to claim social security benefits – in particular housing benefit. After an argument the relationship ended and T maintained that M did not have an interest in the property. She argued that the presumption of a resulting trust was rebutted by the illegal motive.

Although two members of the House of Lords held that the illegal motive prevented M from claiming a share, the majority upheld her claim. They based this on the fact that M could assert ownership without relying on the illegal motive but instead relying on the resulting trust which arose in her favour.

Lord Browne-Wilkinson

'Where the presumption of resulting trust applies, the plaintiff does not have to rely on the illegality. If he proves that the property is vested in the defendant alone but the plaintiff provided part of the purchase money, or voluntarily transferred the property to the defendant, the plaintiff establishes his claim under a resulting trust unless either the contrary presumption of advancement displaces the presumption of resulting trust or the defendant leads evidence to rebut the presumption of resulting trust.'

The formal transfer of rights in land usually involves certain formalities such as the need to satisfy s 2 LP(MP)A 1989 but in some cases an implied trust will be imposed in order to give effect to the intentions of the parties which does not require any formalities.

Under s 60(3) Law of Property Act (LPA) 1925 it is provided that in a voluntary conveyance a resulting trust for the grantor shall not be implied merely by reason that the property is not expressed to be conveyed for the use or benefit of the grantee. It was held in *Lohia v Lohia* [2001] WTLR 101 that the effect of the section was to oust the presumption of a resulting trust in a voluntary conveyance. The claimant must raise evidence that there was no intention to make a gift in order to retain an interest in the property.

5.1.2 Presumption of advancement

CA *Warren v Gurney* [1944] 2 All ER 472

A father purchased a house for his daughter prior to her wedding but he kept the title deeds until death. The presumption of advancement was rebutted because if a transfer had been intended then it would be assumed that the title deeds would have been transferred as well.

Traditionally, the presumption of a resulting trust can be rebutted where the advancement is made within certain relationships, e.g. husband to wife, father to child and anyone to a child who is *in loco parentis*.

CA *McGrath v Wallace* [1995] 2 FLR 114

A father purchased a house in the sole name of the son. It was intended that they would live there together. Although the presumption of advancement applied it was rebutted by evidence that they intended that both parties would hold the beneficial interest.

If there is a written declaration of trust, even if it had not been signed by the parties, it could be admitted as evidence of intention which would rebut the presumption of advancement.

The presumption of advancement from husband to wife was criticised in *Pettit v Pettit* by Lord Diplock on the basis that it reflected the most likely intentions of earlier generations of spouses belonging to the propertied classes of a different social era.

The Family Law (Property and Maintenance) Bill was introduced in 2005 proposing the abolition of the presumption of advancement from husband to wife and fiancé to fiancé. This failed after the first reading. More recently it has been suggested that the principle contravenes human rights and would be open to challenge.

5.1.3 Rebuttal of the presumption of resulting trust or advancement by evidence of an illegal purpose

Tinsley v Milligan (above) suggests that an illegal purpose can be ignored if it was not necessary to rely on it in order to support a claim. In that case the fact that M had contributed towards the purchase of the property held in T's name was sufficient to raise the presumption of a resulting trust. The reason for leaving M's name off the title, which was an illegal purpose, could be ignored.

CA *Gascoigne v Gascoigne* [1918] 1 KB 223

A husband leased some land in the name of his wife, with the intention of defeating his creditors. The husband could not recover the land because he would have to rely on an illegal motive.

An illegal motive cannot be used in order to rebut the presumption of advancement.

 CA *Tinker v Tinker* [1970] P 136

A house was purchased by a husband in the sole name of his wife because he intended to prevent his creditors from claiming it if his business failed.

The court held that this evidence could not be used to defeat the presumption of advancement.

Lord Denning MR
'As against the wife, (the husband) wants to say that it belongs to him. As against his creditors, that it belongs to her. That simply will not do. Either it was conveyed to her for her own use absolutely; or it was conveyed to her as a trustee for her husband. It must be one or the other. The presumption is that it was conveyed to her for her own use; and he does not rebut that presumption by saying that he only did it to defeat his creditors.'

 CA *Tribe v Tribe* [1995] 4 All ER 236

A father owned almost all the shares in a private company. He transferred them into the name of his son because he feared that he would be liable to repair certain premises that were occupied by the company. However, the father was never required to carry out the repairs and so the father requested the return of the shares and the court upheld his request.

This case suggests that if property has been transferred for an illegal purpose such as the defeat of creditors then the purpose can be raised where it was never carried out. So, if the creditors were not defeated and had been fully paid then the property can be reclaimed using the original purpose as the evidence to rebut the presumption of advancement.

5.1.4 Loans

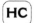 *Re Sharpe (A Bankrupt)* [1980] 1 WLR 219

Property was acquired by the purchaser with the help of a loan from his elderly aunt. When the nephew died the aunt claimed that she had a right to remain there under a resulting trust. Since it had been a loan the presumption of a resulting trust was rebutted.

However, the aunt was able to remain in the property on the basis of an estoppel licence which was binding on the trustee in bankruptcy as a right under a constructive trust. See licences.

Recent cases such as *Stack v Dowden* [2007] (jointly owned property) and *Abbott v Abbott* [2008] (solely owned property) have held that where co-owned property is held in a sole name the interests behind the trust will be held on constructive trust and it is for the court to decide the shares of the parties based on their imputed intentions.

Abbott v Abbott [2007] UKPC 53

'Land was transferred from the husband's mother to a couple soon after their marriage but it was registered in the sole name of the husband. The mother also contributed towards the construction costs although both the husband and wife were liable for the mortgage. After the relationship broke down the husband claimed that it was held on resulting trust thereby giving the wife a share of less than 10 per cent. The court found that it was held on constructive trust for the both husband and the wife.'

5.2 Constructive trusts

5.2.1 The nature of a constructive trust

 Paragon Finance plc v D.B. Thakerar & Co
[1999] 1 All ER 400

Lord Millett
'A constructive trust arises by operation of law whenever the circumstances are such that it would be unconscionable for the owner of property (usually but not necessarily the legal estate) to assert his own beneficial interest in the property and deny the beneficial interest of another.'

The court may impose a constructive trust in a number of situations not because it is giving affect to the intention of the parties but instead to prevent unconscionability.

Bannister v Bannister [1948] 2 All ER 133

The claimant transferred her house to her brother-in-law, the defendant. He gave her an oral undertaking that she was to have a life interest in the property but this was never evidenced in writing as required for a declaration of an express trust of land under s 53 (1)(b) LPA 1925.

The court imposed a constructive trust in favour of the claimant which under s 53(2) LPA 1925 did not require evidence in writing.

It would also be possible to argue that although this was an express trust 'in equity a statute cannot be used as an instrument of fraud' so the lack of writing would not be fatal to the enforcement of the trust. It was on this basis that a trust of land was enforceable in *Rochefoucauld v Boustead* (1897) 1 Ch 196. If property is transferred to someone who knows that it is to be held on trust for another but there is no declaration in writing then the trust will still be upheld. This is based on the principle that equity will not allow a statute to be used an an instrument of fraud.

Reconsider the following case considered earlier under resulting trusts.

 Gissing v Gissing [1971] AC 886 (above)

A couple separated after nearly 30 years of marriage. The husband had purchased a house nine years earlier, using partly his own money and partly a loan from his wife's employer and mainly with the aid of a mortgage. The wife made a number of contributions towards living expenses. In particular, she paid for a new lawn to be laid and also for some items of furniture as well as purchasing clothes for the family and paying towards housekeeping costs. On this basis she claimed she had a beneficial interest and the husband held the property on constructive trust for them both.

The House of Lords held that she had no interest in the property. They could find no evidence of a common intention that the wife was to be entitled to a share of the house.

Lord Diplock
'The picture presented by the evidence is one of husband and wife retaining their separate proprietary interests in the property whether real or personal purchased with their separate savings and is inconsistent with any common intention at the time of the purchase of the matrimonial home that the wife, who neither then nor thereafter contributed anything to its purchase price or assumed any liability for it, should nevertheless be entitled to a beneficial interest in it.'

5.2.2 Evidence of a common intention

 Eves v Eves [1975] 1 WLR 1338

An unmarried couple started living together. The man purchased a house in his sole name, telling the woman, who was aged 19 at the time, that he would have put the house into joint names if she had been 21. He later admitted that this assertion was untrue. However, the court inferred an agreement that the woman was to have an interest in the property. The woman had carried out extensive work on the property, including breaking up a concrete surface with a large sledgehammer; she painted the brickwork in front of the house and demolished a shed with the man and put up a new one in its place. He later left her for another woman and she claimed a share in the house.

The Court of Appeal held that the man held the title on constructive trust for himself and the woman.

If there is a bargain between the parties, either expressly or impliedly, that the claimant is to have a share in the property on account of contributions in kind then the court will give effect to this agreement.

CA *Grant v Edwards* [1986] Ch 638

A man and a married woman whose marriage had broken down started to live together. The man purchased a property and told the woman that he would not put her name on the title deeds because it could prejudice the financial settlement between herself and her husband.

From these facts the Court of Appeal inferred an express common intention to share the beneficial interest. The man had paid the mortgage instalments but the woman made contributions towards housekeeping expenses and caring for the children.

Nourse LJ
'The more difficult question is whether there was conduct on her part which amounted to an acting upon that intention … it is in my view an inevitable inference that the very substantial contribution which the plaintiff made out of her earnings … to the housekeeping and to the feeding and to the bringing up of the children enabled the defendant to keep down the instalments payable under both mortgages out of his income.'

CA *Burns v Burns* [1984] Ch 371

An unmarried couple lived together for over 19 years. The family home was bought in the sole name of the man and the woman made no direct contribution to the purchase. They had two children and she stayed at home to care for them. She only worked when the children were older but her earnings were not used towards the purchase of the property. Instead they were spent on household bills, redecorating the house, which she carried out herself, and buying clothes for the children. The Court of Appeal could find no common intention that she was to derive a share in the property.

May LJ
'When the house is taken in the man's name alone, if the woman makes no "real" or "substantial" financial contribution towards either the purchase price, deposit or mortgage instalments by the means of which the family home was

acquired, then she is not entitled to any share in the beneficial interest in that home even though over a very substantial number of years she may have worked just as hard as the man in maintaining the family in the sense of keeping the house, giving birth to and looking after and helping to bring up the children of the union.'

This case reaffirms the principle that rights in property are dependent on a common intention to share and contributions towards family and general household expenses alone are insufficient to infer such an intention.

 Lloyds Bank v Rosset [1991] 1 AC 107 (above)

A couple purchased a derelict property which required extensive redecoration. Mrs Rosset supervised this work and spent a considerable amount of her time at the property. She undertook aspects of the redecoration herself. The marriage broke down and she claimed a share of the property based on the work that she had undertaken.

The court refused to grant her rights in the property based on her work because it could find no evidence of a common intention to share rights in the property.

Lord Bridge
'There must have been some agreement, arrangement or understanding reached between them that the property is to be shared beneficially.

It was common ground that Mrs Rosset was extremely anxious that the new matrimonial home should be ready for occupation before Christmas if possible. In these circumstances it would seem the most natural thing in the world for any wife, in the absence of her husband abroad, to spend all the time she could spare and to employ any skills she might have, such as the ability to decorate a room, in doing all she could to accelerate progress of the work quite irrespective of any expectation she might have of enjoying a beneficial interest in the property.

… The finding of an agreement or arrangement to share … can only be based on evidence of express discussions between the parties, however imperfectly remembered and however imprecise their terms may have been.

… In this situation direct contributions to the purchase price by the partner who is not the legal owner, whether initially or by payment of mortgage instalments, will readily justify the inference necessary to the creation of a constructive trust. But, as I read the authorities, it is at least extremely doubtful whether anything less will do.'

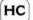 *Le Foe v Le Foe* [2001] 2 FLR 970

The wife had made a small direct contribution towards the purchase of the matrimonial home and over a period of time she had made small contributions towards household expenses.

Relatively small contributions towards household expenses could be seen as indirect contributions towards the purchase price and this also could give rise to evidence of a common intention that one party was to have a share in the property. The important feature is that the contributions allow the husband to pay the mortgage instalments. This point had been made earlier in *Gissing v Gissing* where the House of Lords was agreed that the wife would have then acquired a share.

As can be seen, the courts have not always been prepared to find evidence of a common intention and any claim based solely on contributions in kind will be unsuccessful in spite of criticism from academics and lawyers alike. This can be particularly difficult for a claimant who is a cohabitant and who cannot make a claim for a share in the family home under the Matrimonial Causes Act 1973. The Law Commission has addressed the problems of financial support for cohabitants and in 2007 published a Report 'Cohabitation: The Financial Consequences of Relationship Breakdown'. After several years of research it has proposed a scheme which gives certain cohabitants the right on separation to apply for various kinds of financial relief including lump sums, property transfer and property settlements. If such a scheme were to be adopted, then the role of constructive trusts would be reduced in determining the property rights of a cohabiting couple.

5.3 Assessing the shares in resulting and constructive trusts

Midland Bank plc v Cooke [1995] 4 All ER 562

The parties had been married for nearly 25 years. The house had been purchased in the sole name of the husband but the court found that the wife had contributed 7 per cent towards the purchase price based on her share of the initial deposit paid by her parents-in-law as a joint wedding present. The court had to assess the size of her share. Throughout their marriage they had shared finances and the court took this to infer an intention to share the property equally and so the wife was awarded a 50 per cent share in the property based on the initial contribution of 7 per cent.

In a resulting trust the courts traditionally quantify the shares according to the size of the initial contributions. By contrast, in a constructive trust the courts determine the shares according to any express agreement or by inferring intention from the conduct of the parties.

In this case it was admitted in court by the claimant that there had been no agreement about ownership of the property but this did not affect the wife's claim. The court was prepared to infer such an intention.

Waite LJ
'It would be anomalous … to create a range of home-buyers who were beyond the pale of equity's assistance in formulating a fair presumed basis for sharing of beneficial title, simply because they had been honest enough to admit that they never gave ownership a thought or reached any agreement about it'.

Drake v Whipp **[1996] 1 FLR 826**

CA

A couple purchased a barn, intending to convert it into a house. It was purchased in the man's sole name and he paid the majority of the costs of the conversion. The woman paid towards the purchase price. This represented about 40 per cent of the purchase price but only 20 per cent of the purchase price and conversion costs combined.

The court found this to be a constructive trust because there was a common understanding between the parties that they were to share beneficially. The court could then look at all relevant factors and found that the woman should be entitled to a one-third share. This was based on such factors as their joint bank account and the contributions made to general family expenses and that they intended to share the family home.

CA *Cox v Jones* [2004] 2 FLR 1010

A couple purchased some property in the name of the man, mainly because the woman could not raise a loan in her sole name. She did not pursue separate funding after the purchase had taken place. For over a year the woman supervised building works at the property. The woman was a barrister and the court took into account that her role supervising the building work had affected the progress of her career.

The woman was awarded a quarter share in the property. The supervisory role in the building work constituted detriment.

In what way are the facts of this case different from those of *Lloyds Bank v Rosset* (1991) (above)?

CA *Oxley v Hiscock* [2004] EWCA Civ 546

An unmarried couple purchased a property to provide themselves with a home. The property was purchased in the sole name of Mr Hiscock but the purchase price was provided in part by Mrs Oxley, partly by Mr Hiscock and partly by way of a mortgage. The court found that Mr Hiscock held on constructive trust for Mrs Oxley based on their common intention to share. Although there had been initial contributions which would suggest a resulting trust, the court looked at this as a constructive trust and applied a broader approach to quantification of shares.

The court then reconsidered how courts in all implied trusts will quantify shares. It decided that shares in implied trusts should be based on fairness: 'That share which the court considers fair having regard to the whole course of dealing between them in relation to the property'. The course of dealing would involve looking at such things as contributions to expenses such as housekeeping, utilities and repairs. When these much broader factors were applied the claimant Mrs Oxley was awarded 40 per cent of the property.

This case suggests that quantification of shares has moved away from the strict approach in resulting trusts based purely on the size of contributions. Today the court will look at the whole course of dealing, even in a case based on a resulting trust.

HL ### *Stack v Dowden* [2007] 2 AC 432

Property was purchased in the names of two cohabitants Ms Dowden and Mr Stack. The title was registered in joint names but they did not indicate on registration whether they wished to hold the beneficial interest as joint tenants or tenants in common. The parties had made unequal contributions towards the purchase price which was also funded by a mortgage. Ms Dowden had contributed 65 per cent of the purchase price. When the couple split up the woman claimed a larger share of the property. Since the parties had kept their finances rigidly separate and Ms Dowden had contributed much more to the purchase than Mr Stack the presumption of equality was rebutted.

It was not appropriate to apply a resulting trust to cases of property ownership between husband and wife and cohabitant and cohabitant and it was preferable to apply a constructive trust in such circumstances.

Common intention can readily be implied from the sheer fact of joint legal ownership. In such cases equity follows the law and equity is equality so the law will presume that the beneficial interest will be shared equally. However, this presumption is rebuttable by proof that a contrary inference is to be drawn. The factors that would be proof of a contrary indication could include the reasons why the home was purchased in joint names, the nature of the relationship, the financing of the purchase, the discharge of various finances and other factors.

Baroness Hale
'… when a couple are joint owners of the home and jointly liable for the mortgage, the inferences to be drawn from who pays for what may be very different from the inferences to be drawn when only one is owner of the home. The arithmetical calculation of how much was paid by each is also likely to be less important. It will be easier to draw the inference that they intended that each should contribute as much to the

household as they reasonably could and that they would share the eventual benefit or burden equally ...'

In a dissenting judgment Lord Neuberger sought to uphold the presumption of the resulting trust in deciding shares in a jointly owned property but this presumption could be displaced by evidence of a constructive trust if there was evidence of an agreement supported by detrimental reliance at the time of acquisition. He suggested that such evidence must be substantial such as capital repayments to the mortgage or substantial improvements to the home.

This case is considered later under co-ownership. Where co-owned property is registered at the Land Registry the parties may declare their ownership of the equitable estate. This declaration is optional and where the parties have chosen to remain silent on this matter the court may infer the ownership of the beneficial title from circumstances.

PROPRIETARY ESTOPPEL

DEFINITION
Ramsden v Dyson (1866)
If someone builds on your land and you ignore it, you cannot later assert your title over the land
Taylor Fashions Ltd v Liverpool Trustees Co Ltd (1982)
A claim for proprietary estoppel is based on proof of an assurance; detriment and reliance
THE REPRESENTATION
Crabb v Arun District Council (1976)
A right of way cannot be denied to the claimant if you have built relying on the provision of access
Inwards v Baker (1965)
A representation of rights in land will be binding on a third-party purchaser
Taylor v Dickens (1998)
A promise of rights in a will does not constitute a representation
Gillett v Holt (1998)
A promise of rights in a will can constitute a representation where there has been detrimental reliance
Pascoe v Turner (1979)
An oral representation of rights in land can constitute a representation in spite of no formal transfer of rights
Thorner v Major (2009)
To establish proprietary estoppel the assurance has to be sufficiently clear and this will depend on the context of the assurance. Proprietary estoppel can be upheld where there is a continuing pattern of conduct over a significant period of time
RELIANCE ON THE REPRESENTATION
Greasley v Cooke (1980)
Detrimental reliance can be continuing to provide free services instead of looking for a new job
Re Basham (1986)
A number of incidents of detriment may jointly be sufficient
DETRIMENTAL RELIANCE
Sledmore v Dalby (1996)
Where both parties suffer detriment the courts will balance their claims
Coombes v Smith (1986)
Detriment can be ignored if there has been no assurance of rights
THE REMEDY
Jennings v Rice (2003)
The remedy should be proportionate to the assurance given
Williams v Staite (1979)
Misconduct by the claimant is irrelevant where estoppel has been established
E. R. Ives Investmant v High (1967)
If a benefit is claimed over land the burden is also carried
Yeoman's Row Management v Cobbe (2008)
An oral commercial arrangement that is binding in honour only cannot usually generate a claim under proprietary estoppel
Pascoe v Turner (1979)
The courts awarded the transfer of the legal estate
Greasley v Cooke (1980)
Grant of a right to occupy property rent-free for the remainder of the claimant's life
Dodsworth v Dodsworth (1973)
Grant of monetary compensation rather than a right to remain in the property

6.1 Definition

HL *Ramsden v Dyson* (1866) LR 1 HL 129

Lord Kingsdown

'If a stranger begins to build on my land supposing it to be his own, and I perceiving his mistake, abstain from setting him right, and leave him to persevere in his error, a court of equity will not allow me afterwards to assert my title to the land on which he had expended money on the supposition that the land was his own.'

Until 1982 proprietary estoppel relied on proof of five *probanda* laid down in *Willmott v Barber* (1880) 15 Ch D 96:

i) claimant of an equity makes a mistake about his/her legal rights;

ii) on the basis of the mistake the claimant acts to his/her detriment by spending money or carrying out some act;

iii) knowledge by the possessor of the legal right of the other party's belief;

iv) knowledge by the other party that the belief is mistaken;

v) the other party must have encouraged the claimant in the expenditure incurred.

HC *Taylor Fashions Ltd v Liverpool Trustees Co Ltd* [1982] 1 QB 133

A 28-year lease had been granted to the predecessors in title of the claimants, Taylor Fashions. It carried an option to renew for a further 14 years. The option had not been registered because the claimants mistakenly believed that it was not necessary and as a result it was not binding on the third party purchasers of the freehold title. After taking possession of the property the claimants had carried out extensive improvements to the property with the consent of the landlords. Taylor Fashions claimed that the landlords were estopped from denying the exercise of the option to renew, even though it had not been registered, because they had known of the improvements made by the claimants.

The court rejected the claim and upheld the defendants' right to refuse to renew the lease.

The court took the opportunity to review the law on proprietary estoppel. It rejected the five *probanda* laid down in *Willmott v Barber* and simplified the rules on proprietary estoppel.

Today a claim for proprietary estoppel must be based on proof of the following: an assurance, detriment and reliance.

It is rare today for the five *probanda* of *Wilmott v Barber* to be used. There are occasional references, eg *Matharu v Matharu* (1994) 68 P & CR 93.

6.2 The representation

CA *Crabb v Arun District Council* [1976] Ch 179

The defendant decided to sell part of his land. He had reached agreement with the Council that he should have a right of way over some Council land preventing his reserved plot from becoming landlocked. This agreement was never confirmed in writing. On this basis he sold part of his plot but the Council then refused him access.

The Council could not deny him rights because it had led him to believe that he would be granted rights of way and that had led him to act to his detriment in selling part of his land without reserving an easement in his favour.

Lord Denning

'(the doctrine of estoppel) ... seeks to prevent a person from insisting on his strict legal rights – whether arising under a contract, or on his title deeds, or by statute – when it would be inequitable for him to do so having regard to the dealings which have taken place between the parties.'

Inwards v Baker [1965] 2 QB 29

A son intended to buy some land in order to build a bungalow. His father persuaded him to build on land belonging to him but there was no formal conveyance of the land. The son believed that he would have the right to remain on the property during his lifetime but when the father died he discovered that others had inherited the property.

Although there was no formal conveyance to him the court upheld the son's rights and granted him the right to remain in the property during his lifetime based on the representation made to him by the father.

Taylor v Dickens [1998] 3 FCR 455

An elderly lady promised her gardener that she would leave her estate to him. He continued to help her with work around the house without pay.

The court held that he was not entitled to claim a share of her estate after her death based on estoppel because she had not at any time suggested to him that she would not exercise her right to change her will before death.

 Gillett v Holt [2001] Ch 210

Promises were made to the claimant over a period of time that he would be left a share of the estate. The claimant had worked for over 40 years for the defendant.

Walker LJ
'In this case Mr Holt's assurances were repeated over a long period, usually before the assembled company on special family occasions.'

 Pascoe v Turner [1979] 1 WLR 431

The defendant and the claimant were not married. She moved in with him at first as his housekeeper but this later developed into a relationship and he represented to her that she could regard his house as belonging to her. This representation was made orally and so could not be a formal transfer of rights.

His promise was held to be a representation on which the claimant had acted to her detriment and she was entitled to a remedy.

***Thorner v Major* [2009] UKHL 18**

The claimant worked on his cousin's farm over a period of thirty years without payment but with an expectation of eventually inheriting the farm. Although the Court of Appeal held that the claimant's case should fail because the representation was not sufficiently clear, the House of Lords upheld his claim.

Lord Neuberger
'The courts should not be "unrealistically rigorous" in applying the "clear and unambiguous" test.'

6.3 Reliance on the representation

***Greasley v Cooke* [1980] 1 WLR 1306**

The claimant had been a maid working for a family. She had stayed with the family for nearly 30 years, having begun a relationship with one of the sons of the family. During this time she had looked after a mentally ill member of the family and cared for the house, having been assured that she could stay there all her life.

The court regarded the fact that during this time she did not look for another job as detrimental reliance on the promises made to her.

Lord Denning
'Suffice it that she stayed on ... in ... the house – looking after Kenneth and Clarice – when otherwise she might have left and got a job elsewhere.'

HC *Re Basham* **[1986] 1 WLR 1498**

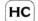

The claimant and her husband cared for her step-father for a period of many years. He led them to believe that he would leave his entire estate to the claimant when he died.

Although most of the incidents relied on in support of the claim were non-financial and would not in themselves be very significant, taken together they 'went well beyond what was called for by natural love and affection': Edward Nugee QC.

6.4 Detrimental reliance

CA *Sledmore v Dalby* **(1996) 72 P & CR 196**

The defendant son-in-law had lived in a house owned by his mother-in-law rent-free for 12 years since his wife had died. He claimed that his wife had been promised the house by her parents prior to her death and, combined with the various improvements that he had made over the years, he argued that he had acted to his detriment relying on these promises.

His mother-in-law sought possession of the house.

The court overturned the earlier decision of the High Court and made an order in favour of the mother-in-law based on surrounding issues of the case. These include the fact that he had alternative accommodation and his children were all grown up and only used the property for part of the week. By contrast, his mother-in-law was elderly and she could no longer afford to live in her present home and needed the house to live in. In granting the remedy the court considered the proportionality between the remedy and the detriment which it sought to avoid. In the circumstances it was fairer to uphold the mother-in-law's claim.

C *Coombes v Smith* [1986] 1 WLR 808

This case concerned a couple who were both married to other partners. A house was purchased in the name of the man and the woman moved in and started immediately to decorate it. The man never moved in with her, even when she moved to another house again purchased in his name. He then started a relationship with another woman and she claimed rights in the house based on estoppel.

Her claim was refused on the basis that she was not assured of property rights by the man when she first moved into his house. So neither the act of leaving her husband, nor having a child and caring for it nor decorating the property could constitute detrimental reliance.

The courts seem to have taken differing views as to what can constitute an assurance and also what constitutes detriment. Compare the approach taken in *Coombes v Smith* (1986) with other cases such as *Re Basham* (1986) and *Pascoe v Turner* (1979).

6.5 The remedy in estoppel

6.5.1 Satisfying the equity

CA *Jennings v Rice* [2003] 1 P & CR 8

The claimant had cared for an elderly lady although he was not related to her. She had led him to believe that he would get a share in her estate, possibly her house and the furniture – which were valued at approximately £400,000, and even the entire estate valued at over £1 million.

The court awarded him £200,000 which was the equivalent of full-time nursing care. It thought that a higher award would be disproportionate to the assurances given.

Robert Walker LJ

'The equity arises not from the claimant's expectations alone, but from the combination of expectations, detrimental reliance, and the unconscionableness of allowing the benefactor (or the deceased benefactor's estate) to go back on the assurance.'

Jennings v Rice establishes that in estoppel cases the court is seeking to preserve some kind of proportionality between the detriment which has been incurred by the estoppel claimant and the remedy which the court awards. This will also take into account any benefit which the claimant may have also received from the promisor.

6.5.2 Transfer of the legal estate

Pascoe v Turner [1979] 1 WLR 431

The courts awarded the transfer of the legal estate.

6.5.3 Grant of a right to occupy

Greasley v Cooke [1980] 1 WLR 1306

The claimant was granted a right to occupy the property rent-free for the remainder of her life.

6.5.4. Grant of monetary compensation

Dodsworth v Dodsworth (1973) 228 EG 1115

Grant of monetary compensation rather than a right to remain in the property.

6.5.5 If a benefit is claimed over land a reciprocal burden may also be carried

ER Ives Investment Ltd v High [1967] 2 QB 379

The defendant had accepted that the foundations of the claimant's flats which had been wrongly placed on the defendant's land could remain. In return, the claimant had allowed the defendant the right of access to his garage at the rear of his house across the claimant's land. The right could have existed as an equitable easement but it had not been registered by the defendant. The claimant then tried to prevent access but the court upheld the rights of the defendant under the principle of estoppel.

The rights of the defendant were upheld on the principle of 'he who takes the benefit must take the burden'.

Consider this principle in relation to positive covenants in **Chapter 11** and the rule in *Halsall v Brizell*.

6.5.6 Misconduct by the claimant

CA *Williams v Staite* [1979] Ch 291

The defendants had been given the right to occupy two cottages indefinitely. They also used a paddock which they had no right to use and they even built a stable on the land. Although the court grant prevented them from using the paddock they could not be prevented from enjoying the cottages.

The court did not take misconduct by the claimant into account when considering an appropriate remedy where estoppel had been successfully established.

LICENCES

TYPES OF LICENCE

Thomas v Sorrell (1673)
No proprietary rights arise under a licence but it will confer legality on an action

A LICENCE COUPLED WITH AN INTEREST OR GRANT

Hurst v Picture Theatres Ltd (1915)
A licence coupled with a grant is not revocable by the licensor
Hounslow LBC v Twickenham Garden Development Ltd (1971)
An 'interest' in land includes the right and duty to do works on land

CONTRACTUAL LICENCES

Wood v Leadbitter (1845)
A contractual license can be revoked at any time by the licensor and the licensee's remedy lies in damages
Winter Garden Theatre (London) Ltd v Millennium Productions Ltd (1946)
Reversed the principle in *Wood v Leadbitter*. A contractual licence cannot be revoked whilst the contract subsists
Verrall v Great Yarmouth BC (1981)
The remedy for breach of a contractual licence in land can be specific performance
Tanner v Tanner (1975)
Consideration for a contractual licence includes giving up rights under a protected tenancy

ESTOPPEL LICENCES

Inwards v Baker (1965)
Greasley v Cooke (1980)
Rights arising under estoppel constitute licences in land

THE EFFECT ON THIRD PARTIES

King v David Allen & Sons (Billposting) Ltd (1916)
A licence cannot constitute a proprietary right on land
Clore v Theatrical Properties Ltd (1936)
A purely personal right cannot bind third parties acquiring rights in property
Errington v Errington & Woods (1952)
Binions v Evans (1972)
A contractual licence can bind a third-party purchaser
Ashburn Anstalt v Arnold (1989)
A contractual licence cannot bind a third-party unless there is evidence of a constructive trust
Re Sharpe (1980)
Where rights arise under licence and a constructive trust only those under a constructive trust will be binding

7.1 Types of licence

 CA *Thomas v Sorrell* (1673) Vaughan 330

Vaughan CJ

'A dispensation or licence properly passeth no interest, nor alters or transfers property in anything, but only makes an action lawful without it had been unlawful.'

7.1.1 Licences coupled with an interest

 CA *Hurst v Picture Theatres Ltd* [1915] 1 KB 1

The claimant was forcibly ejected from a cinema although he had earlier bought a ticket. He brought an action in trespass against the cinema owners based on his right to remain on the premises.

If a licence is coupled with a grant of an interest it is not revocable by the licensor whereas a mere licence can be revoked at any time and the licensee merely has time to leave the premises before becoming a trespasser.

Buckley LJ

'If the facts here are as I think they are … that the licence was a licence to enter the building and see the spectacle from its commencement until its termination, then there was included in that contract a contract not to revoke the licence until the play had run to its termination. It was then a breach of contract to revoke the obligation not to revoke the licence.'

Hounslow LBC v Twickenham Garden Development Ltd
[1971] Ch 233

The defendants started building works on the claimant's land.
The claimants became dissatisfied with the defendant's standard
of work and they tried to terminate their contract and as a result
asked them to leave their land. The defendants argued that the
conditions of the contract had not been broken.

It was held that as long as the contract subsisted, the
defendants had a right to be on the claimant's land.

An 'interest' is not confined to an interest in land or in
chattels and it could include the right to attend a creditors'
meeting or to see a cinema performance as well as the right
and duty to do works on land.

Megarry J
'A licence to go on land to sever and remove trees or hay, or to
remove timber or hay that have already been severed are
accepted examples of a licence coupled with an interest.'

7.1.2 Contractual licences

 Wood v Leadbitter (1845) 13 M &W 838

The claimant had bought a ticket to attend the races at
Doncaster. This entitled him to attend for four days. He was
forcibly ejected before the end of the race meeting and he

claimed that he had an irrevocable licence to remain on the premises for the entire four days and was entitled to damages for assault. It was held that he could claim damages for breach of contract but the court held that the licence was revocable and so once revoked the claimant became a trespasser which meant he was not entitled to damages.

A contractual licence is a licence granted for value such as the right to park in a car park. The extent of the rights conferred by a contractual licence is governed by general contractual principles. Some rights will be implied and others will be expressly agreed between the parties.

 CA/ HL *Winter Garden Theatre (London) Ltd v Millennium Productions Ltd* [1946] I All ER 678

The defendants granted the claimants a licence to use their theatre for the production of plays, concerts or ballets for six months. They also held an option to renew the contract which they chose to exercise. The defendants then tried to revoke their licence although the claimants were not in breach of their contract.

The Court of Appeal held that whilst the contractual licence can be revoked at any time under common law under equity a contractual licence may be irrevocable.

The case went on appeal to the House of Lords and it was held that construction of this contract the licence was intended to be revocable. It was never intended that the licence should be irrevocable. The House of Lords concluded that there was an implied term allowing the licensor to terminate the licence after a year by a reasonable period of notice. The House of Lords concluded that Lord Greene was correct in saying that a licence should not be regarded as separate from the contract.

 Verrall v Great Yarmouth BC [1981] QB 202

The Great Yarmouth Borough Council had agreed with the National Front that they could use the Wellington Pier for their annual conference. The Labour Party gained control of the Borough Council and tried to revoke the National Front's licence. The Court of Appeal granted an order for specific performance to the claimants.

As the remedy lay in equity it was therefore discretionary. In this case the special factor that the claimants could not find another venue at such short notice allowed the court to unusually order specific performance rather than merely award damages.

 Tanner v Tanner [1975] 1 WLR 1346

A woman gave up valuable rights under a protected tenancy to come to live with the defendant, who was the father of her twin children, in property which he owned in his sole name. When the relationship broke down she claimed the right to continue to live in the property based on a contractual licence.

The court held that she could claim rights under a contract which would allow her to live in the property at least whilst the children were of school age and they needed accommodation.

When these rights were unlawfully terminated she could claim a sum in damages to compensate her for loss of her rights.

7.1.3 Estoppel licences

An estoppel licence arises in favour of the licensor by means of the doctrine of proprietary estoppel.

Many of the cases considered under proprietary estoppel will be relevant here. Consider *Inwards v Baker* [1965] 2 QB 29 (above) where the son, who had been urged by his father to build a bungalow on the father's land, was granted an irrevocable licence to live there after the father's death. The court adopted a similar approach in *Greasley v Cooke* [1980] 1 WLR 1306 when a maid who had cared for a family and had been encouraged to believe that she could live in the property all her life was granted a right to remain in the property during her life.

7.2 The effect of licences on third parties

HL *King v David Allen & Sons (Billposting) Ltd* [1916] 2 AC 54

The defendants granted the claimants a contractual licence to put up posters and advertisements on the wall of a cinema when it had been built. Once built, the cinema was leased to a company who then refused the claimants the right to put up the posters. The House of Lords refused to enforce the licence against the third-party company.

The licence was a purely personal right between the parties

and only enforceable in contract. It was not a proprietary right in land.

Is there any reason why a contractual licence should not be enforceable as a right in land? There have been a number of attempts, mainly by Lord Denning, over the years to try to confer proprietary status on contractual licences.

CA *Clore v Theatrical Properties Ltd* [1936] 3 All ER 483

The claimants had been granted exclusive rights to provide refreshments in a theatre by the lessors. The agreement used the terms 'lessor' and 'lessee' and held that the terms 'lessee' and 'lessor' should include their executors, administrators and assigns. The assignee of the lessor then sought to prevent the claimants from continuing with their right to provide refreshments.

The court held that the right was a personal covenant only and this would not be binding on the third party assignees. It was held that the agreement was not a lease but a licence only.

CA *Errington v Errington and Woods* [1952] 1 KB 290

A man purchased a house for his son and daughter-in-law, which he told them they would own provided that they paid the mortgage instalments. The instalments constituted two-thirds of the purchase price. He promised them that the house would be theirs when the mortgage had been paid off. After the father's death the son deserted his wife and his mother, who now owned the cottage, tried to recover possession from her daughter-in-law.

It was held that the contractual licence of the daughter-in-law was binding on the mother.

The judge in *Errington* was Lord Denning who sought to confer proprietary status on contractual licences. He argued that notice of the licence would render them binding on the purchaser. Although he was successful in *Errington* it was short lived and the House of Lords refused to enforce the personal rights of a wife against a mortgagee in *National Provincial Bank Ltd v Ainsworth* (1965). However, he continued to support the principle in subsequent cases but usually without the support of his fellow judges.

CA *Binions v Evans* **[1972] Ch 359**

A defendant had remained in a cottage in which she had lived rent-free with her husband whilst he was employed on the Tredegar Estate. On his death she was given the right to continue living there as tenant-at-will, rent-free, for the remainder of her life on condition that she kept the cottage in good repair and cared for the garden. The claimants purchased the estate and tried to evict her. The Court of Appeal held that her rights bound the claimants since they had purchased the cottage subject to her rights and at a reduced price.

The three judges in the Court of Appeal all agreed that her rights were binding, but they did not agree on what basis the defendant could claim the right to live in the property.

Only Lord Denning decided the case on the basis of a contractual licence, and the fact that this could give the occupier an equitable interest in the land and prevent the purchaser from turning the occupier out if he bought with knowledge of her right. He also suggested that where a purchaser bought with knowledge of rights then he would be bound by those rights as constructive trustee.

 Re Sharpe [1980] 1 WLR 219

A nephew bought a house with the help of an elderly aunt and he agreed that she could live with him and his wife and be cared for by them. The nephew suffered financial difficulties and later went bankrupt and the property vested in his trustee in bankruptcy who sought possession of the house. The aunt claimed the right to remain in the house.

The aunt had the right to continue to live in the property although the judge, Mr Justice Browne-Wilkinson, was uncertain on which grounds her rights could be upheld. He based his judgement on both an estoppel licence and also a constructive trust but concluded that only the constructive trust would be binding on the trustee in bankruptcy

In the later case of *Ashburn Anstalt v Arnold* (1989) (below) the court doubted whether the rights of the aunt did constitute rights under a constructive trust but the aunt was still entitled to an irrevocable licence to occupy until the loan was repaid under proprietary estoppel.

CA *Ashburn Anstalt v Arnold* [1989] Ch I

This case reviewed the law on the status of contractual licences. The owner of a shop sold it to a developer subject to a right that he could remain there, rent-free, until the redevelopment took place. A third-party purchaser argued that this right did not bind him because it was a licence.

A contractual licence would not bind a third party unless there was evidence of a constructive trust. Fox LJ considered what evidence would lead one to conclude that there was a constructive trust. Certainly, evidence that the purchaser had bought at a reduced price would be sufficient to suggest that the rights should be upheld, but to purchase merely with notice of the rights would not give rise to a constructive trust although to buy expressly giving effect to third party rights will raise a constructive trust.

CHAPTER 8

CO-OWNERSHIP

EXPRESS DECLARATION
Goodman v Gallant (1986)
An indication of equitable ownership on the conveyance will be binding
Stack v Dowden [2007]
Failure to indicate on documents of registration whether the equitable estate is held as a joint tenancy or tenancy in common is not conclusive and the law will presume that the legal owners will hold the property on trust for themselves as joint tenants

OTHER EVIDENCE OF EQUITABLE OWNERSHIP
Malayan Credit Ltd v Jack Chia-MPH Ltd (1986)
Partners in business hold an equitable estate in property as tenants in common
Other evidence of a tenancy in common includes purchase in unequal shares; security for a loan

SEVERANCE OF A JOINT TENANCY
(i) Statute
Re Draper's Conveyance (1969)
A joint tenancy is severed where written notice is served satisfying s 36(2) LPA 1925
Harris v Goddard (1983)
No severance unless an immediate desire to sever is shown
(ii) Severance by post
Kinch v Bullard (1998)
Once a letter has been delivered there is effective severance under statute
Re 88 Berkeley Road (1971)
A recorded letter constitutes severance under s 196(4) LPA 1925 if the letter has not been returned by the post office
Gore and Snell v Carpenter (1990)
An agreement to sever is not effective unless it is intended to take effect immediately
(iii) Common law
Burgess v Rawnsley (1975)
Negotiations over severance can be sufficient under common law even where agreement has not been reached
First National Securities Ltd v Hegerty (1985)
An act of alienation of a share can constitute severance
Re Dennis (1993)
A trustee in bankruptcy acting for a husband could claim the entire property after the death of the wife

FORFEITURE
Re K (Deceased) (1985)
The Forfeiture Act 1982 allows the court to modify the operation of the forfeiture rule where hardship could result

8.1 Express declaration of trust of co-owned land

Goodman v Gallant [1986] 1 All ER 311

A wife jointly owned the matrimonial home and her new partner purchased her former husband's share with financial help from the wife. The conveyance declared that the two would be beneficial joint tenants. After that relationship broke down the wife claimed a three-quarter share in the property based on her half-share and the financial assistance that she gave to her partner.

Where the conveyance expressly states that property is to be held under a joint tenancy it is irrelevant that there are other features such as contributions in unequal shares that would indicate a tenancy in common.

Stack v Dowden [2007] 2 AC 432

Where the legal estate in land is held by more than one person and it has not been indicated on the registration of the title whether the parties hold as joint tenants or tenants in common, then it is presumed that equity will follow the law and they will hold as joint tenants. However, this presumption can be rebutted with contrary evidence and the presumption was rebutted in this case.

8.1.1 Partners in business

Malayan Credit Ltd v Jack Chia-MPH Ltd
[1986] AC 549 (PC)

The parties had taken a lease of business premises as joint tenants at law. They agreed that each party would occupy a specific part of the premises and pay rent and expenses *pro rata*. There was no express agreement as to the nature of the tenancy.

A joint tenancy at law cannot be severed but there could be a tenancy in common in equity under three circumstances:

i)   where they have purchased in unequal shares;
ii) where the grant consists of a security for a loan;
iii) where they are business partners and the subject-matter for the grant is partnership property.

In this case they were partners in a business and the courts found evidence of a tenancy in common in equity.

8.2 Severance under statute

HC **Re Draper's Conveyance** [1969] 1 Ch

A husband and wife divorced in 1965. Together they jointly owned the matrimonial home under an express trust. The wife sought an order for the sale of the house with the proceeds to be shared between them. Before the case was heard the husband died intestate. The Court found that there was severance under s 36(2) LPA 1925. The issue of the summons clearly showed an intention to sever immediately.

The joint tenancy will be severed once written notice which satisfies s 36(2) LPA 1925 is served on the other joint tenants showing an immediate desire to sever, and not a desire to sever sometime in the future.

Plowman J

'The written notice clearly evinced an intention on the part of the wife that she wished the property to be sold and the proceeds distributed, a half to her and a half to the husband.'

Harris v Goddard [1983] 1 WLR 1203

A husband and wife split up and the wife started divorce proceedings. She stated in her petition that she wanted the court to make 'such order in relation to the matrimonial home as may be just' and this was to include either transfer of the home or settlement of the property or variation of existing trust interests. Three days before the petition was heard the husband was injured in a car crash and later died.

The court held that the joint tenancy had not been severed. There was no severance because no immediate desire to sever, necessary for s 36(2) LPA 1925, was shown in the papers.

8.3 Severance by post

Kinch v Bullard [1998] 4 All ER 650

A couple owned the matrimonial home as joint tenants in law and in equity. The wife petitioned for divorce and sent a letter to her husband by ordinary post, indicating her intention to sever the joint tenancy. The following day he had a heart attack and was rushed to hospital. The letter was delivered to the house whilst he was in hospital. The wife intercepted the letter and decided to destroy it because she considered that her husband now had a possible chance of dying in the next few months and although she herself was ill she anticipated that she would outlive him. Eventually both parties died and the court had to consider whether the letter had severed the joint tenancy in spite of the fact that the wife had changed her mind and withdrawn her agreement.

Once the letter had been delivered there was effective severance under statute, and it was too late for the joint tenant to have a change of mind. Therefore the husband's share passed under the terms of his will and did not automatically pass to the wife under the survivorship rules.

Neuberger J
'Provided that it can be established that irrespective of the identity of the person who delivered the notice to a particular address, it was delivered to that address, then the notice has been validly served at that address.'

What if the letter had been intercepted before delivery? Then might it have been possible for severance to be withdrawn? The wife might have been able to withdraw the letter from the postman before delivery.

 Re 88 Berkeley Road [1971] Ch 648

A house was purchased by two single women, Miss Goodwin and Miss Eldridge, who held the property as joint tenants. Miss Goodwin sent a notice to Miss Eldridge, who was to marry in a few weeks, that she intended to sever her interest in the property. This was sent by recorded delivery which expected acknowledgement of receipt of the notice. As Miss Eldridge was away on holiday the acknowledgement was by Miss Goodwin who had sent the notice. Miss Goodwin died soon after this and her executors claimed that there had been severance. It was claimed on behalf of Miss Eldridge that as she had not received the notice there had not been proper severance.

As the letter was sent by recorded delivery, s 196(4) applied. This held that notice has been served if a letter had been sent by recorded post and had not been returned to the post office. The fact that the party intending to sever had signed for the recorded letter did not affect the issue of severance.

HC *Gore and Snell v Carpenter* (1990) 60 P & CR 456

A husband and wife decided to split up. Together they were beneficial joint tenants of two houses. One solicitor drew up a separation agreement dealing with the property and, in particular, the draft agreement included a severance clause in relation to their interests in the matrimonial home. However, there was no specific attempt to sever the joint tenancy before the husband died and the separation agreement had not been fully agreed.

The court did not find severance because the parties had not reached agreement and there was no evidence of an immediate intention to sever.

Blackett-Ord J
'A course of dealing is where over the years the parties have
dealt with their interests in the property on the footing that
they are interests in common and are not joint.'

8.4 Severance under common law

8.4.1 Severance under *Williams v Hensman* (1861)

Williams v Hensman (1861) 1 John & H 546

KJ Page-Wood VC
'... A joint tenancy may be severed in three ways: in the first
place, an act of any one of the parties interested operating
upon his share may create severance of that share ... Secondly,
a joint tenancy may be severed by mutual agreement. And, in
the third place, there may be severance by any issue of dealing
sufficient to intimate that the interests of all were mutually
treated as constituting a tenancy in common...'

8.4.2 Fraudulent transfer of the entire interest by a joint tenant

CA | ***First National Securities Ltd v Hegerty*** [1985] QB 850

A couple purchased a house jointly. The house was to be their
home for retirement. Before they moved in the husband left
his wife. He raised money on a mortgage but did not tell his
wife and he forged her signature on the documentation.

It was held that this was an act of alienation and had severed the joint tenancy and the husband and wife were held as tenants in common. This protected the share of the wife from the mortgagee.

CA *Burgess v Rawnsley* [1975] Ch 429

A couple met at a scripture rally in Trafalgar Square. They became friends and as a result jointly purchased a house. It was expressly declared in the conveyance that they held as joint tenants. The relationship did not develop and Mr Honick offered to buy Mrs Rawnsley's share. They discussed this but disagreed about the price. At Mr Honick's death the price was still undecided. It was held that the doctrine of survivorship did not apply and the joint tenancy was held to have been severed at common law. Mrs Rawnsley could only claim a one-half share in the property. The other half went to Mr Honick's daughter who succeeded to his estate.

The Court of Appeal decided that the joint tenancy had been severed at common law under mutual agreement. There had not been agreement as to the exact price but there was sufficient negotiation for the court to find that there had been mutual agreement about the sale and a course of mutual dealing and thereby severance under common law.

Re Dennis [1993] Ch 72

A couple owned two houses as joint tenants in law and equity. In September 1982 the husband committed an act of bankruptcy and a few months later in December a bankruptcy petition was presented. In February 1983 the wife died and the husband was adjudicated bankrupt in November 1983.

It was held that the property only vested in the trustee in bankruptcy on the adjudication of bankruptcy.

In this case the tenancy had not been severed on the wife's death so the husband held the entire interest on the death of his wife under the doctrine of survivorship. As a result the trustee in bankruptcy was entitled to claim both houses.

See Gore and Snell v Carpenter (1990) 60 P & CR 456

The court did not find mutual conduct as there were simply negotiations between the husband and wife and ... there was no finality and there was no mutuality.

8.5 Forfeiture

 Re K (deceased) [1985] Ch 85

A couple had been unhappily married for many years. The wife had suffered from continuous and grave domestic violence. One evening they had a serious fight and the husband was killed by a shot from a loaded shotgun. It was fired accidentally by the wife and found to be a tragic accident.

Where one joint tenant is responsible for the death of the co-tenant the court will usually hold the tenancy to be severed and refuse to uphold the principle of survivorship. In this case, by applying s 2(1) of the Forfeiture Act 1982 and because of the special circumstances of this case, survivorship was held to apply.

Section 2 of the Forfeiture Act allows the court to modify the operation of the forfeiture rule which prevents survivorship from taking effect. It will take into account the conduct of the offender and of the deceased and other material circumstances. However severance has been held to have taken place in some cases where the surviving joint tenant had aided and abetted suicide which is contrary to the law under the Suicide Act 1961.

CHAPTER 9

TRUSTS OF LAND

The effect of a trust of land

Bull v Bull (1955)
A beneficiary under a trust has a right to occupy the property

The purpose of the trust

Re Buchanan Wollaston's Conveyance (1939); *Jones v Challenger* (1961)
Sale of property held on trust for sale can be delayed while the purpose of the trust exists
Bedson v Bedson (1965)
If one of two purposes for the trust still exists, sale can be delayed
Re Evers Trust (1980)
Use as a family home can be a reason to postpone sale

Sale under the Trusts of Land and Appointment of Trustees Act 1996

Mortgage Corporation v Shaire (2001)
The court has a greater degree of flexibility when considering whether or not to postpone sale under s 15 TOLATA than under the old law
Rodway v Landy (2001)
s 13 TOLATA allows the count to partition trust property
Bank of Ireland Home Mortgages v Bell [2001]
In exercising its discretion whether or not to order sale it should always be a 'powerful consideration' whether a secured creditor was receiving proper consideration for being kept out of his money

Repairs by a co-trustee and payment of rent

Leigh v Dickeson (1884)
A co-tenant cannot ask for a contribution towards repairs from another co-tenant unless he first agrees
Dennis v Macdonald (1982)
A co-tenant is entitled to rent from the co-tenant if the threat of violence forces them to leave the trust property

Bankruptcy

Re Citro (1991)
Exceptional circumstances under the Insolvency Act 1986 does not include young children and the need to change schools
Re Holliday (1981)
Sale can be delayed under the Insolvency Act 1986 where the husband petitioned for bankruptcy himself
Barca v Mears (2005)
Nicholls v Lan (2007)

9.1 The effect of a trust over land

Bull v Bull [1955] 1 QB 234

Property was purchased jointly between a mother and her son in the name of the son. Contributions were unequal but it was accepted that the son held the equitable estate as trustee on behalf of them both as tenants in common. They lived in the property together, but later when the son married he asked his mother to leave. It was held that the mother as a co-owner under a trust had a right to live in the property.

Co-owners are both entitled to occupy and enjoy land. This right cannot be denied to one co-owner by the other co-owner. So a beneficiary under a trust had the right to occupy the property whilst the trust subsisted. This case was decided before the Trusts of Land and Appointment of Trustees Act (TOLATA) 1996. Under the old law trusts for sale placed an obligation on the trustees to sell the property. Today the trust of land places no such obligation, however, even under a trust for sale, the beneficiaries had the right to remain in the property until sale.

Denning MR
'(T)he son, although he is the legal owner of the house, has no right to turn his mother out. She has an equitable interest which entitles her to remain in the house as tenant in common with him until the house is sold.'

9.2 The purpose of the trust

Re Buchanan-Wollaston's Conveyance [1939] Ch 738

Four owners who were all neighbours joined together to buy a piece of land which they wanted to keep as an open space. The land was conveyed to them as joint tenants. One of the four wanted to sell the land and the other three resisted the application.

Under the law at the time, the land was held under a trust for sale. Sale could be delayed whilst the original purpose of the trust existed and it was held that whilst three of them wanted to keep the land the purpose of the original trust for sale still subsisted.

Jones v Challenger [1961] 1 QB 176

After their marriage had broken down the wife sought an order for sale of the former matrimonial home; the husband defended the claim, arguing that the purpose of the trust still existed – namely to provide a home for the parties to the marriage. The court made an order for sale on the basis that this purpose no longer existed.

Under the law pre-1996 applications to the court for an order for sale were governed by consideration of whether or not the purpose behind the trust still subsisted.

CA *Bedson v Bedson* [1965] 2 QB 666

A property was purchased in joint names of a husband and wife to provide a home for them both, and also premises for the husband's drapery business. The purchase price was wholly provided by the husband. On the breakdown of the marriage the wife sought an order for sale through the court.

The court refused to order sale on the basis that the original purposes of the trust still subsisted, namely to provide premises for a shop and also living accommodation for them both.

 CA *Re Evers Trust* [1980] 1 WLR 1327

A couple purchased a family home. They were unmarried and they lived with one son of the relationship and two sons from the woman's previous marriage. When the relationship broke down the court postponed an order for sale. They held that sale might be ordered where the wife remarried or when she was in a position to buy the man's share in the property or when the child of the relationship reached 18.

Sale was postponed in this case because the original purpose of the trust was still being carried out – namely to provide a home for the children.

The previous cases were all decided on the law as it existed prior to the 1996 Act. In *Mortgage Corporation v Shaire* (below)

Neuberger J considered their relevance in the light of the new act. He concluded that it would be wrong to 'throw over the wealth of learning and thought given by so many eminent judges' but the law had undergone an important change and so there could be dangers in relying on earlier authorities. He concluded that these cases were to be treated with caution.

HC *Bank of Ireland Home Mortgages v Bell* **[2001] 2 All ER 920**

The court ordered the sale of property although there was still a minor living there and the original purpose to provide a family home had not been discharged.

Although under s 15 TOLATA 1996 no one factor is to be considered by the court above all others, the court held that the interests of the secured creditors and whether or not they were entitled to their money was a powerful consideration.

9.3 Sale under the Trusts of Land and Appointment of Trustees Act 1996

HC *Mortgage Corporation v Shaire* **[2001] Ch 743**

Mrs Shaire and Mr Fox purchased a house in joint names as tenants in common with Mrs Shaire owning a 75 per cent share and Mr Fox a 25 per cent share. Mr Fox secretly took out a mortgage forging Mrs Shaire's signature. Mr Fox later died and the mortgagees sought an order for sale to realise his share of the property. In applying s 15 TOLATA 1996 and having considered the interests of any secured creditors the court postponed sale.

Under s 15 TOLATA 1996 the court has a greater degree of flexibility when considering whether or not to postpone sale of the property.

Neuberger J
'The 1996 Act has the effect of rendering a trust for sale obsolete, including those in existence on January 1 1997 and replacing them with the less arcane and simpler trusts of land.'

Consider whether the courts might choose to rely on earlier authorities where the facts are closer such as *Eves v Eves* and *Jones v Challenger* rather than the special circumstances of *Mortgage Corporation v Shaire*.

9.4 Other applications under the Trusts of Land and Appointment of Trustees Act 1996

CA *Rodway v Landy* **[2001] Ch 703**

A partnership between two doctors was wound up. The doctors owned their premises jointly and one doctor, Dr Rodway, sought an order that the premises be sold, but his partner, Dr Landy, wished to continue in practice and sought an order under s 13 TOLATA 1996.

The Court of Appeal held that they had power under s 13 to

make an order allocating different parts of a building for exclusive occupation by different beneficiaries, particularly as the premises were such that they could be partitioned and split between the two partners. They also found that it was possible under the section to require a beneficiary to pay any costs needed to make the physical separation possible.

Gibson LJ

'On any footing before 13 allows the trustees to divide a building subject to a trust of land between two out of three or more beneficiaries entitled to occupy, and also, if I am right, between the only beneficiaries entitled to occupy. It would be surprising if the cost of adapting the building to make each part suitable for separate occupation of the beneficiary could not be imposed on the beneficiary.'

9.5 Repairs by a co-trustee and the payment of rent

CA *Leigh v Dickeson* (1884) 15 QBD 60

One co-tenant incurred expenses for repairs and improvements which he had voluntarily and unilaterally decided to carry out. He demanded contributions from his co-tenants.

Where a co-tenant spends money on repairs and improvements of the co-owned property he is not entitled to ask for a contribution from the other co-tenant except under certain limited circumstances: such as where the co-tenant has requested or agreed to the improvements or they have both agreed that they must be carried out. However on the sale of the property it may be possible to claim an equitable lien on the property which represents the increased value of the property after the improvements have been carried out.

 Dennis v Macdonald [1982] Fam 63

The claimant had been forced to leave the family home because of the violence and threatened violence of the defendant. She was therefore unable to exercise her right as a co-owner to occupy the family home. The defendant was ordered to pay her an occupation rent equivalent to half the fair rent for an unfurnished letting.

It was held that he had to pay her compensation since she was denied the right to occupy the property a right which all co-owners have. However, where tenants in common choose not to exercise their right to occupy property then they are not entitled to claim rent from their co-tenant. In cases where the tenant in common is unable to enjoy the property because she has, in the circumstances, been excluded from the matrimonial home then unusually rent may be ordered from the co-tenant still in occupation.

Purchas J
'Therefore the basic principle that a tenant in common is not liable to pay an occupation rent by virtue merely of his being in sole occupation of the property does not apply in the case where an association similar to a matrimonial association has broken down and one party is, for practical purposes, excluded from the family home.'

9.6 Applications to sell trust property in bankruptcy

CA *Re Citro* [1991] Ch 142

An application was made for sale against the jointly owned family home by a trustee in bankruptcy. The wife applied for the sale to be deferred on the basis that the children were young and as a consequence of the sale would be forced to move schools. The court considered s 335A of the Insolvency Act 1986 which lists the matters which the court has to consider before making an order for sale. These included the interests of the husband's creditors, the conduct of the spouse or former spouse, the needs and financial resources of the spouse or former spouse, the needs of any children and all the circumstances of the case other than the needs of the bankrupt. However, after one year the court must assume that the needs of the creditors outweigh all other considerations unless the circumstances of the case are exceptional.

The age of the children and the fact that they had to change schools were not seen to be exceptional circumstances under s 335A of the Insolvency Act 1986 and so an order for sale was made.

Nourse LJ
'Where a spouse with a beneficial interest in the matrimonial home has become bankrupt under debts which cannot be paid without the realisation of that interest, the voice of the creditors will usually prevail over the voice of the other spouse and a sale of the property ordered within a short period. The voice of the other spouse will only prevail in exceptional

circumstances.'

Re Holliday (A bankrupt) [1981] Ch 405

The matrimonial home was owned jointly by a husband and wife. The husband left the wife and she continued to live in the property with their three children. He then petitioned for his own bankruptcy and the husband's trustee in bankruptcy sought an order for sale.

The Court of Appeal accepted that there were exceptional circumstances and exercised its discretion by refusing an order for sale. The exceptional circumstances included the fact that there were very young children, the husband had petitioned for his own bankruptcy and his creditors could all be paid without having to sell the property.

Barca v Mears [2005] 2 FLR 1

A bankrupt argued that the special educational needs of his son were exceptional circumstances under s 335(A) Insolvency Act 1986. He also argued that the interpretation of 'exceptional circumstances' was contrary to art 1 of the First Protocol and article 8 of the European Convention on Human Rights.

It was held that these rights were not absolute and in most cases sale will be necessary for the protection of the rights of others. In this case the needs of the creditors could only be protected by sale.

HC *Nicholls v Lan* [2007] 1 FLR 744

The bankrupt's wife was a chronic schizophrenic and moving from her home was likely to cause her extreme difficulty. Nevertheless although the court regarded these factors as exceptional the court only delayed an order for sale for eighteen months rather than indefinitely.

The court balanced her needs with the fact that there were no children of the family and the need for the creditors to be paid sooner rather than later.

This case suggests that the courts will construe exceptional circumstances very narrowly.

9.7 The effect of overreaching

 HL *City of London BS v Flegg* [1988] AC 54 (above)

Here, property was purchased in the name of a daughter and her husband. Her mother and father had also both contributed money but their rights took effect in equity. The husband took out a mortgage which he could not repay and the building society sought to sell the property. The rights of the parents were transferred to the capital monies, which had been dissipated by the son so they were left with nothing.

The rights of co-owners can be transferred from rights in the land to rights in the rents and profits arising on sale. Their rights are said to be overreached and this will only occur where there are two trustees of land. S. 27(1) LPA 1925.

Consider how this case affects the beneficiaries' statutory right to occupy under a trust of land.

Overreaching will only apply where there are two trustees. Reconsider *Williams & Glyn's Bank v Boland* (1981) under registered land (**Chapter 4**) where Mrs Boland's rights were not overreached because the capital monies were paid to a sole owner – namely Mr Boland.

CHARACTERISTICS OF AN EASEMENT

Re Ellenborough Park (1956)
i) The dominant and servient tenement must be owned by two different people
ii) The easement must accommodate the dominant tenement
iii) There must be a dominant and servient tenement
iv) The right must be capable of forming the subject-matter of a grant
Hill v Tupper (1863)
A right unconnected with the use of land cannot be an easement
Moody v Steggles (1879)
A benefit to land can include business use if it benefits the land, not the business
Copeland v Greenhalf (1952)
Rights amounting to possession of land cannot be easements
Wright v Macadam (1949)
A right of storage can exist an an easement
London & Blenheim Estates Ltd v Ladbroke Retail Parks Ltd (1992)
The right to park can exist as an easement
Moncrieff v Jamieson and others (2007)
A right of vehicular access may carry with it a right to park if it was necessary for the enjoyment of the easement
Greatorex v Newman (2008)
A right of way created for business premises over residential property was limited to the owner and it did not automatically confer rights for customers except in an emergency
Virdi v Chana and another (2008)
An easement must not prevent any use by the landowner of his land but an easement may be upheld even if it severely limits the potential use of a landowner's property

IMPLIED EASEMENTS

The rule in Wheeldon v Burrows
Wheeldon v Burrows (1879)
A quasi-easement can be converted into an easement if it is continuous and apparent and it is necessary for the reasonable enjoyment of the property and in use at the time of grant

s62 LPA 1925
International Tea Stores v Hobbs (1903)
Licences can be converted into easements on the conveyance of land
Goldberg v Edwards (1950)
Any right for the benefit of land can pass as an easement under s 62

COMMON INTENTION
Wong v Beaumont Property Trust Ltd (1965)
The trust will imply an easement to give effect to the common intention of the parties

NECESSITY
Barry v Haseldine (1952)
The court will imply an easement of necessity if the land does not have an independent right of access
Wheeler v JJ Saunders (1995)
A claim for an easement of necessity will fail if there is an alternative means of access
Stafford v Lee (1993)
An easement of necessity could be implied for woodland where the original deed showed the land could be used for housing

PRESCRIPTION
Mills v Silver (1991)
An easement can arise under prescription if:
i)   the use of the land is without force, secrecy or permission;
ii) it is enjoyed by a fee simple owner against another fee simple owner;
iii) the use is continuous

Union Lighterage Company v London Graving Dock Company (1902)
An easement through prescription will not arise unless the use is open

EXCESSIVE USE
Jelbert v Davis (1968)
If increased use is excessive than it will be restrained
British Railways Board v Glass (1965)
Increased use of a right is lawful if it is contemplated at the grant

10.1 Characteristics of an easement

CA *Re Ellenborough Park* [1956] Ch 131

A number of owners of land claimed that the right to enjoy a piece of neighbouring land for leisure purposes could exist as an easement.

This case establishes that a right can exist as an easement if it satisfies the following conditions:

i)   the owners of the dominant and servient tenements must be two different people;

ii) the easement must accommodate the dominant tenement (it must provide a benefit to the land rather than a personal advantage to the owner of the land;

> iii) there must be a dominant and servient
>   tenement;
> iv) a right cannot amount to an easement unless it
>   is capable of forming the subject-matter of a grant.

10.1.2 The easement must accommodate the dominant tenement

 Hill v Tupper (1863) 2 H & C 121

The claimant Hill had a lease of an area of land next to a canal. He had the sole right to put boats on the canal and when the defendant Tupper who owned an inn which bordered the canal also put boats onto the water Hill claimed that his rights had been infringed.

It was held that the claimant did not have an easement but merely a licence.

A right that is unconnected with the use and enjoyment of land cannot exist as an easement.

 Moody v Steggles (1879) 12 Ch D 261

The owners of a pub put up an advertising sign on the wall belonging to a neighbouring house. Their claim that this right existed as an easement was upheld.

If an easement benefits land then the fact that the land is used as a business cannot defeat the claim that it exists as an easement.

10.1.3 The right cannot amount to an easement unless it is capable of forming the subject-matter of a grant

HC *Copeland v Greenhalf* [1952] Ch 488

A wheelwright unsuccessfully claimed that the right to store vehicles awaiting repair on a narrow strip of land existed as an easement.

The right could not exist as an easement because the claimant claimed rights over the whole strip of land which amounted to possession of the land itself.

Upjohn J
'I think that the right goes wholly outside any normal idea of an easement, that is the right of the owner ... of a dominant tenement over a servient tenement. This claim ... really amounts to a claim to a joint user of the land by the defendant.'

CA *Wright v Macadam* [1949] 2 KB 744

The claimant was a tenant in an upper-storey flat in a house. She claimed that the right to use the coal shed to store her coal passed to her as an easement rather than continuing as a mere licence on the renewal of her lease. She was successful in spite of the possibility that it involved the exclusive use of the shed.

HC *London & Blenheim Estates Ltd v Ladbroke Retail Parks Ltd* [1992] 1 WLR 1278

The claimant, who owned a large shopping centre, claimed that his customers had the right to park on a central car park and such a right could exist as an easement.

The right to park on the land of another can exist as an easement unless it would leave the servient owner without any reasonable use of his land, whether for parking or anything else.

CA *Batchelor v Marlow* [2001] EWCA Civ 1051

An easement by prescription was claimed over the claimant's land by the defendants to park and store six cars between 8.30 am and 6.00 pm Monday to Friday. There was room on the land for only six cars. The Court of Appeal found no easement existed because it would deprive the owner of any reasonable use of his land.

It is difficult to reconcile *Wright v Macadam* with *Copeland v Greenhalf*. These decisions were highlighted in the later case of *London & Blenheim Estates Ltd v Ladbroke Retail Parks Ltd*. Judge Paul Baker saw it is a matter of degree whether a right which involved exclusive occupation of part of the servient tenement could exist as an easement. He suggested that a small coal shed in a large property was one thing (*Wright v Macadam*) and the exclusive use of a large part of the alleged servient tenement was another (*Copeland v Greenhalf*).

HL | *Moncrieff v Jamieson and others* [2007] 1 WLR 2620

The claimant lived on one of the Shetland islands in Scotland. He had a vehicular easement over his neighbour's land. He also claimed a right to park cars on the servient land because without this right the easement would have been 'effectively defeated'.

An easement of a right to park could be constituted as ancillary to a servitude right of vehicular access if it was necessary for the enjoyment of the easement of access. It was sufficient that it might have been in contemplation at the time of grant having regard to what the dominant proprietor might reasonably be expected to do in the exercise of his right to convenient and comfortable use of the property.

CA | *Greatorex v Newman* [2008] EWCA Civ 1318

The owner of a public house claimed that his customers had

the right to use a right of way enjoyed by the owner. It was held that the use exceeded the right granted to the owner and the customers could only use it in time of emergency.

***Virdi v Chana and another* [2008] EWHC 2901 (Ch)**

The occupiers of property had parked their car on adjoining land for over 20 years and claimed a right under prescription. The owners of the adjoining land challenged their claim on the basis that it prevented them from use of their own land and could not therefore lie in grant.

It was held that the easement could take effect as the amount of the landowner's property that was claimed was too small to be of practical use to him. Where the landowner has little value in use of his/her property an easement which severely limits his/her potential use will not debar the existence of an easement.

10.1.4 The right must not impose a positive burden on the servient owner

***Crow v Wood* [1971] 1 QB 77**

A right to have the servient land fenced, or a fence or wall kept in repair, has been held to be an easement. In this form it imposes an obligation on the servient landowner to take positive action.

Chapter 10 Covenants
A positive covenant cannot be enforced against a successor in title but it may be enforceable as an easement of fencing.

10.2 The grant of an easement

10.2.1 The rule in *Wheeldon v Burrows*

 Wheeldon v Burrows (1879) 12 Ch D 31

 A parcel of land was split between the owner and a purchaser, Wheeldon. The owner sold part of his land which included a workshop to Burrows. Hoardings were erected on Wheeldon's land which interfered with the light in the workshop. Burrows maintained that the right to light existed as an easement and so the hoardings must be taken down.

It was held that an easement existed.

 The rule in *Wheeldon v Burrows* can convert a quasi-easement into an easement when certain conditions apply:

i) the right must have been exercised by the owner continuously and apparently. This means it must be obvious to anyone that such a right is enjoyed, e.g. a right of way;
ii) the right must be necessary for the reasonable enjoyment of the property;
iii) the right must be in use at the time of grant.

 Wheeler v JJ Saunders Ltd [1995] 2 AER 97

The claimants owned a farmhouse that had previously enjoyed a right of access over the defendant's land, as well as an alternative means of access. The defendants built a wall blocking off the right of way and the claimants argued that

they had an easement under *Wheeldon v Burrows*. They were
unsuccessful because they had an alternative means of access.

A claim for the grant of an easement under *Wheeldon v
Burrows* will fail if the claimant has an alternative means of
access. It will only succeed if the right can be shown to be
necessary for the reasonable enjoyment of the property.

10.2.2 Implied easements under s 62 Law of Property Act 1925

HC | *International Tea Stores Co v Hobbs* [1903] 2 Ch 165

The claimant bought the dominant tenement which he had
previously leased from the defendant. Prior to the purchase he
had permission to use a short-cut across the defendant's land.
It was held that this right of use now existed as an easement.

Rights that exist as licences over neighbouring land can become
converted into easements when the land is conveyed to the
claimant. This is because the effect of s 62 LPA 1925 allows the
grantee automatically to acquire the benefit of an easement and
any rights attaching to the land that are listed in the section,
even if they are not expressly mentioned in the conveyance.

CA | *Goldberg v Edwards* [1950] Ch 247

The dominant land was owned by the defendants. They
granted a lease of an annex adjoining the land to the claimants.
The claimants moved into the premises and started using the

front door for access even before the lease had been executed. Although there was an alternative means of access the claimants claimed that this right had passed to them under the lease.

Any right enjoyed for the benefit of land and that is capable of existing as an easement will pass under s 62.

It is important when applying s 62 to distinguish between those rights enjoyed for the benefit of the land, in which case the right will pass, and rights that are personal to the claimant which do not pass either to the licensee or to a third party when the land is conveyed.

Wright v Macadam (above)

In this case the right to store coal passed to the widow on the renewal of her lease under s 62 even though the original right was a licence. This was because the right of storage is regarded as conferring a benefit on land and the court regarded it as capable of existing as an easement.

10.2.3 Common intention

 Wong v Beaumont Property Trust Ltd [1965] 1 QB 173

The claimant leased basement premises to be used as a Chinese restaurant. The landlord knew it needed ventilation to comply with public health regulations but he would not allow the tenants to fix a duct on his land which would then enable a ventilation system to be fitted. However, the court held that this right existed as an easement and the landlord could be forced to agree.

The court will imply an easement where it is necessary to give effect to the common intention of the parties to a grant of land for the use of that land. The use must be definite at the moment of the grant and not a mere possibility. In this case the lease limited the use of the basement to a restaurant but it could not open as a restaurant without the use of the ventilation system.

 Stafford v Lee (1993) 65 P & CR 172

An area of woodland and a pond were conveyed to the claimant's predecessors in title. This land fronted a private drive that had access to the main road but the conveyance did not mention any rights of access over the drive. The claimant decided to develop the land and claimed an easement over the road. The defendants challenged this right, arguing that an easement could not be inferred because the land had only been used as a woodland and therefore did not require a right of way for cars.

As the original deed had been accompanied by a plan which had shown use of neighbouring land for houses then such an easement could be inferred here.

10.2.4 Necessity

 Barry v Haseldine [1952] Ch 832

The purchaser bought land that was completely surrounded by land belonging to the grantor and others. The purchaser exercised access over a disused airfield with permission of its owner but he had no legal right of access for his land.

The court implied an easement of necessity over the grantor's land because the land purchased did not have an independent right of access.

10.3 Prescription

10.3.1 Rights acquired under prescription

CA *Mills v Silver* [1991] Ch 271

The defendants purchased a derelict farm and the only access was a track across adjoining land that belonged to the claimants. There was no express grant of this right but the claimants were aware of it. Later the claimants tried to prevent the defendants from using the track. The court held an easement had been acquired through prescription, based on the doctrine of lost modern grant.

For an easement to arise under prescription, three things must be proved:

i)   the right to use the land must be enjoyed without force, secrecy or permission;
ii) the use must be in fee simple, i.e. the right must be enjoyed by a fee simple owner against an owner of fee simple servient land;
iii) the use must be continuous and this is a question of degree.

Union Lighterage Company v London Graving Dock Company [1902] 2 Ch 557

The defendant had fixed the side of his dock, using tie rods, to land which belonged to the claimant. The rods used had held the wooden walls of the appellant's dock in place for over 20 years. The defendant claimed that he had acquired an easement through prescription under the doctrine of lost modern grant.

An easement could not rise through prescription because the tie rods of the defendant had been buried in the ground and therefore challenged one of the key requirements of prescription, namely that the right should be exercised openly.

10.4 Excessive use

Jelbert v Davis [1968] 1 WLR 589

An easement had been acquired over agricultural land. The original conveyance provided 'the right of way at all times and for all purposes over the driveway ... leading to the main road, in common with all other persons having the like right'. At a later date a change of use was granted allowing the land to be used for caravans and camping. This considerably increased the use of the access road.

The increased use was excessive and an injunction was granted restraining the use by the caravans and campers although the previous more limited use was still available.

CA *British Railways Board v Glass* [1965] Ch 587

A farmer who owned some land adjoining a railway line had acquired the right to cross the railway line through prescription. It allowed him to cross with 'all manner of cattle'. Several caravans on his land used this right. After a number of years this use increased from six caravans to 30.

The increased use was not one contemplated by the original grant and it was not a change of use so the application for an injunction was refused.

CHAPTER 11

COVENANTS

THE NATURE OF COVENANTS

Austerberry v Corporation of Oldham (1885)

A burden cannot be enforced in law against a successor in title to the covenantor

Smith & Snipes Hall Farm Ltd v River Douglas Catchment Board (1949)

The benefit of a covenant will pass to successors if:

(i)   the covenant touches and concerns the land;

(ii)   the original covenantee had a legal estate;

(iii) the successor has a legal estate;

(iv) the benefit was intended to run.

P & A Swift Investments v Combined English Stores Group (1989)

A covenant guaranteeing the performance of covenants 'touches and concerns the land'

Roake v Chadha (1984)

The benefit of a covenant will not run if a contrary intention is shown

---

COVENANTS AT LAW

Rhone v Stephens (1994)

The original convenator will continue to be bound by the burden of a covenant

Halsall v Brizell (1957)

The burden of a covenant can run if the successor takes a benefit under the covenant

COVENANTS IN EQUITY

Tulk v Moxhay (1848)

A burden of a covenant in equity will run against a successor if 1) it is restrictive and 2) it is intended to run and the 3) successor has notice of it 4) it touches and concerns the land

LCC v Allen (1914)

The original covenantee must have owned land for a benefit to run

STATUTORY ANNEXATION

Federated Homes Ltd v Mill Lodge Properties Ltd (1980)

s 78 LPA 1925 allows the benefit of a covenant to be automatically annexed to land

---

BUILDING SCHEMES

Elliston v Reacher (1908)

A covenant will run under a building scheme even where the original covenantee does not retain any land

REMEDIES FOR BREACH OF COVENANT

Wrotham Park Estate Co Ltd v Parkside Homes Ltd (1974)

The remedy for breach of covenant lies in equity and is discretionary

Wakeham v Wood (1982)

An injunction may be granted to demolish a single-storey building built in breach of covenant

Jaggard v Sawyer (1995)

Damages for breach of covenant are compensatory and not restitutionary

11.1 The nature of covenants

CA | ***Austerberry v Corporation of Oldham***
(1885) 29 Ch D 750

 The claimant and defendant were successors in title to the original covenantee and covenantor of a covenant which contained an obligation to keep a road in good repair. It was held that neither the benefit nor the burden had passed at law.

 The law will not enforce a burden against a successor in title to the original covenantor, although the original covenantor himself will remain liable under the covenant.

 How can the law ensure that essential covenants, which benefit land, continue to be enforceable between neighbours and their successors in title?

CA | ***Smith & Snipes Hall Farm Ltd v River Douglas Catchment Board*** [1949] 2 KB 500

The defendants entered into a covenant with a number of owners of land including the claimant's predecessor in title Mrs Smith, agreeing to carry out works to limit the threat of flooding by improving and maintaining the river bank. The claimants wanted to enforce the covenant against the defendants. This depended on whether the benefit of the covenant had passed to them.

The benefit of the covenant had passed to them as successors in title to the original covenantee because certain requirements were fulfilled:

i)   the covenant touched and concerned the land;
ii) the original covenantee had a legal estate in the land benefited;
iii) the successor in title had acquired a legal estate in the land;
iv) the benefit of the covenant was intended to run with the land.

 HL *P & A Swift Investments v Combined English Stores Group* [1989] AC 632

This case concerned leasehold covenants, but the principles are relevant to freehold covenants. The defendant acted as surety for a sub-tenant. It was questioned whether assurances given by the surety that a sub-tenant would perform covenants could run with the land.

The House of Lords held that if the surety's covenant is to guarantee the performance of a sub-tenant's covenants which touch and concern the land then the surety covenant 'must itself be a covenant which touches and concerns the land'.

 HC *Roake v Chadha* [1984] 1 WLR 40

A restrictive covenant was executed between the parties in 1934. It stated that no more than one house would be built on a plot of land and added 'this covenant shall not enure for the benefit of any of any owner or subsequent purchaser of any part of the … estate unless the benefit of this covenant shall be expressly assigned'. The issue was whether this qualification prevented the benefit of a covenant from automatically running with the land.

The benefit of a covenant will usually run at law if the conditions in *Smith & Snipes Hall Farm Ltd v River Douglas Catchment Board* are complied with but where there is a contrary intention shown in the wording of the deed then the benefit cannot pass. It is still possible for the parties to require express assignment of a covenant, in which case it must be assigned each time the property changes hands and at the same time as each change of ownership occurs.

11.2 Covenants at law

Prior's Case (1368) YB 42 Edw III

A positive covenant that a prior and his convent would sing all week in the covenantee's chapel was upheld, notwithstanding the fact that there was no servient tenement to carry the burden.

HL *Rhone v Stephens* [1994] 2 AC 310

A roof that was only accessible from the covenantor's house, overhung the covenantee's property. The original covenantor had sold the property and his successor in title refused to undertake repairs as agreed under the covenant. The House of Lords refused to enforce the positive burden. An argument that the obligation on the owner of the house to maintain the roof was a burden linked with the benefit of rights of support from the neighbouring cottage failed.

The successor in title to the original covenantor will not be bound in law by covenants entered into with a covenantee. The original covenantor will continue to be bound and if he can be found he can be sued where the covenant has been broken.

HC *Halsall v Brizell* [1957] Ch 169

A deed granted rights to use roads and drains to those occupying property on a housing estate. It included an obligation to contribute towards the expenses of maintenance and this was disputed.

It was argued that the burden of a positive covenant could not run at law or in equity but the judge applied an ancient rule of law that 'a man cannot take the benefit under a deed without subscribing to the obligations thereunder'.

CA *Thamesmead Town v Allotey* (2000) 79 P & CR 557

The defendant was relieved of the payment of maintenance costs in respect of certain facilities because they related to facilities that he did not use and he therefore derived no benefit.

The rule in *Halsall v Brizell* constitutes an exception to the rule in *Austerberry v Corporation of Oldham* (above) which prevents the burden of covenants running at law.

Consider *ER Ives Investment Ltd v High* [1967] 2 QB 379 and connected issues of estoppel and licences.

11.3 Covenants in equity

CA *Tulk v Moxhay* (1848) 2 Ph 774

Mr Tulk owned land in Leicester Square and when he sold it to Mr Elms a covenant was entered into that Mt Elms would maintain the land as an open square. Mr Moxhay purchased the square from Mr Elms and, although he knew about the covenant, tried to build on the land. Mr Tulk sought to enforce the original covenant against Mr Moxhay arguing that he had actual notice of the original covenant and so could not ignore it. The court held that the covenant was enforceable.

In certain circumstances the burden of a covenant will be enforceable against successors in title of the original covenantor:

i) the covenant must be restrictive in nature;
ii) the covenant must have been entered into to run with the land;
iii) the covenant must be one that touches and concerns the land;
iv) the successor must have purchased with notice of the covenant. The covenant must either be entered by notice on the Charges Register (in registered land) or as a Class D ii land charge in the event of the land being unregistered.

CA *London County Council v Allen* [1914] 3 KB 642

The owner of land entered into a covenant that he would not build on a plot at the end of new road. This was not enforceable against the successor in title of the covenantor because the London County Council who were the original covenantees did not own any land in the area.

A restrictive covenant will only accommodate a dominant tenement if the original covenantee owned some land to take the benefit at the date when the covenant was granted. Further, a covenant can only be enforced if the dominant tenement claiming the covenant enjoyed sufficient physical proximity with the servient tenement.

11.3.1 Statutory Annexation

Crest Nicholson Residential (South) Ltd v McAllister
[2003] 1 All ER 46, [2004] 1 WLR 2409

A covenant 'not to use the premises for any purpose other than those of or in connection with a private dwelling house' was granted when land was sold off in separate plots. Thirty years later a subsequent purchaser wanted to build new houses on the plot and challenged the meaning of the covenant. The issue was whether the covenant meant that only one house could be built on the land or that the plot was to not to be used other than for residential purposes. It was held that the covenant meant that only a single dwelling house could be built on the plot.

Neuberger J
'as a matter of ordinary language, the indefinite article "a" tends to carry with it the concept of a singularity as opposed to plurality' (judgment in the High Court).

Federated Homes Ltd v Mill Lodge Properties Ltd
[1980] 1 WLR 594

 A single developer owned a number of plots of land. One plot named as the blue plot was sold to the defendants who entered into a covenant that they would not build more than 300 houses on it. The claimants later bought another plot called the green land which carried an express assignment of the benefit of the covenant with it and they also bought a further plot, the red land, but that did not carry the express assignment. The issue before the court concerned the red plot and whether the benefit of the covenant over the blue land could be enforced by the owners of the red land.

 The benefit of the covenant had been annexed to the land by operation of s 78 LPA 1925. This section was interpreted in such a way that any covenant relating to land must be read as if made with the covenantor and his successors in title and the persons deriving title under it or them, including the owners and occupiers for the time being of the covenantee's land, and that therefore such a covenant must be regarded as annexed under statute to the land.

 One of the mysteries surrounding this case is why it took so long to construe the meaning of s 78 in this way. Do you consider that the statute intended automatic statutory annexation of the benefit of every freehold covenant?

11.3.2 Express Annexation

 Rogers v Hosegood [1900] 2 Ch 388

A covenant was granted to covenantees who enjoyed an interest in the land benefited as mortgagees, that 'no more than one house would be built on the land'. It was expressly stated in the deed that the covenant was to 'enure for the benefit of the mortgagees, their heirs, and assigns and others claiming under them to all or any of their lands adjoining or near to the premises'.

It was held that this showed an intention that the benefit of the covenant was annexed to the land of the covenantee.

11.4 Building schemes

 Elliston v Reacher [1908] 2 Ch 374

A developer sold a number of separate plots using identical conveyances and imposing identical covenants upon each purchaser. The area had been laid out specifically before sale into separate plots. The issue before the court was whether the covenants were enforceable against the original covenantor.

Covenants can be enforced under a building scheme where the following criteria exist:

i) both vendor and purchaser derive title under a common vendor;

ii) that prior to selling the land the vendor had laid out his estate in lots and all lots were to be subject to the same or similar restrictions;

iii) that the restrictions were intended by the common vendor to be for the benefit of all the lots;

iv) that when each lot was purchased it was on the understanding that the restrictions were to benefit all the lots within the scheme.

There are several benefits in claiming that a building scheme has been established:

i) the covenant will run even though the original covenantor does not retain any land capable of being benefited;

ii) all the purchasers of plots in the scheme can enforce the covenants between themselves irrespective of the date on which they or their predecessors in title bought their plots;

iii) the benefit of the covenant will automatically run to all the successors in title of the original covenantees without express annexation or express assignment. This is less important since the decision in *Federated Homes v Mill Lodge Properties* gave statutory annexation of freehold covenants unless there is a contrary intention shown in the deed.

Subsequent cases such as *Re Dolphin's Conveyance* [1970] Ch 654 and *Baxter v Four Oaks Properties Ltd* [1965] 1 Ch 816 relaxed the rules laid down in *Elliston v Reacher* so it is no longer necessary that all the land has been sold by a common vendor and there may still be a building scheme even where the vendor has not laid out the land in plots before the first land was sold.

11.5 Remedies for breach of a restrictive covenant

HC *Wrotham Park Estate Co Ltd v Parkside Homes Ltd* [1974] 1 WLR 798

A restrictive covenant was agreed, between the servient owners and the dominant owners of two plots of land, that the servient owners would not build on a certain plot of land without first obtaining approval from the dominant owners. In breach of this covenant they began building on the land, and continued in spite of objections raised by the owners of the dominant land.

The judge did not award a mandatory injunction ordering the demolition of the houses in view of the fact that the houses had now been built and demolition would be, in the words of Brightman J, 'an unpardonable waste of much needed houses'. He awarded the dominant owners a sum which was equivalent to 5 per cent of the servient owners' development profits in lieu of an injunction.

CA *Wakeham v Wood* (1982) 43 P & CR 40

The defendant had broken a restrictive covenant by building a small summer home in such a way that the claimant's view of the sea was obstructed. Warnings had been given but had been ignored by the defendant. The Court of Appeal granted a mandatory injunction ordering demolition of the building.

The award of a mandatory injunction will be rare and will only be granted in certain circumstances, e.g. where there has been a 'flagrant disregard of the plaintiff's rights'. Here the actual building was small, unlike the development in *Wrotham Park Estate Ltd* (above).

CA *Jaggard v Sawyer* [1995] 1 WLR 269

The defendant had built a house on a piece of land adjoining his house. He lived on a private estate and everyone was bound by a restrictive covenant that they would not build further houses on their land. Although the covenant did not extend to the new house the other owners sought an order preventing access to the new house via the private road of the estate which was owned by everyone on the estate.

An injunction was refused, both at first instance and also in the Court of Appeal, but damages were awarded and the measure of damages was compensatory, namely what the claimant had lost, rather than restitutionary, i.e. what the defendant had gained. So here it was not the value of the new house but the price the defendant would have paid in order to obtain consent from the claimant.

MORGAGES

RIGHTS OF THE MORTGAGOR

Biggs v Hoddinott (1898)
Collateral advantages are enforceable whilst the mortgage continues
Bradley v Carritt (1903)
A term of a mortgage cannot be enforced after redemption of the mortgage
Kreglinger v New Patagonia Meat & Cold Storage Ltd (1914)
A mortgage term will be upheld if it is not a clog or fetter on redemption
Fairclough v Swan Brewery Co (1912)
A term preventing redemption until weeks before a long lease ends is a fetter on redemption
Knightsbridge Estates Trust Ltd v Byrne (1939)
A term postponing redemption between two businessmen will not be a fetter on redemption
Jones v Morgan (2002)
A provision that the mortgagee could have a share or interest in the property constituted an impermissible clog on the mortgagor's equity of redemption

ORDER FOR SALE

Barrett v Halifax Building Society (1996)
A mortgagor can force sale against the wishes of the mortgagee

UNFAIR TERMS

Multiservice Bookbinding Ltd v Marden (1979)
A mortgage will not be set aside if there is no evidence of unequal bargaining power between two parties; independent advice is given and one party did not take advantage of the other
Cityland & Property (Holding) Ltd v Dabrah (1968)
If the original rate of interest is unfair a court has the power to substitute a new rate
Paragon Finance plc v Nash (2002)
The right to vary interest can only be exercised for proper motives

UNDUE INFLUENCE

Barclays Bank v O' Brien (1994)
A mortgagee will be bound by the mortgagor's rights where he/she enters the mortgage under undue influence
CIBC Mortgages v Pitt (1994)
A mortgagor cannot rely on undue influence if it was not exerted by the mortgagee or his agent
Royal Bank of Scotland Ltd v Etridge (No. 2) (1998)
There can be undue influence even where there had been independent advice but not if the proper steps are observed
Alliance and Leicester plc v Slayford (2001)

> ### RIGHTS OF THE MORTGAGEE
>
> **THE RIGHT OF POSSESSION**
> *Palk v Mortgage Services Funding plc* (1993)
> Even if the mortgagee forces a sale the mortgagor remains liable for outstanding amounts
> *Quennell v Maltby* (1979)
> The right to seek possession of property is not available if the mortgagee is not acting *bona fide*
> *Cheltenham and Gloucester Building Society v Norgan* (1996)
> The timing of repayments will depend on the length remaining of the mortgage
> *Target Homes v Clothier* (1994)
> Possession will be postponed if the mortgagor can show they have a good prospect of selling the property themselves
>
> **THE RIGHT TO SELL**
> *AIB Finance v Debtors* (1998)
> The law puts a duty on the mortgagees to preserve a business before sale
> *Cuckmere Brick Co Ltd v Mutual Finance Ltd* (1971)
> The mortgagee was under a duty to take reasonable care to obtain the true market price for the property
>
> **APPOINTMENT OF A RECEIVER**
> *Medforth v Blake* (1999)
> The receiver owes a duty of due diligence to the mortgagor over the management of premises

12.1 Rights of the mortgagor

12.1.1 Redemption must be free from any clogs or fetters

 Biggs v Hoddinott [1898] 2 Ch 307

The mortgagors were publicans and a term of their mortgage over the public house which they ran, was that the mortgagees would supply all the beer to them. The mortgagors argued that this term was void in equity because it was a clog or fetter on the mortgage.

The covenant did not affect the equity of redemption. The mortgage could be redeemed independently from the covenant. This case suggests that collateral advantages can be enforceable while the mortgage continues.

HC *Bradley v Carritt* [1903] AC 253

A mortgage was drawn up over shares in a tea company. One of the terms was that the mortgagor should use his best endeavours to ensure that the mortgagee, who was a tea broker, should act as agent for the company's tea. The mortgagee tried to enforce this term after the mortgage had ended.

It was held that such a term could not be enforced after redemption.

This case concerns a key issue in mortgages. To what extent are the parties free to include terms that they wish? In *Bradley v Carritt* the court was split 3:2, with the minority in favour of allowing business the freedom to negotiate bargains without intervention from the courts. It may have been different here if the term was a purely personal one and did not relate to the property at all.

HL *Kreglinger v New Patagonia Meat & Cold Storage Co Ltd* [1914] AC 25

A firm of meatpackers borrowed £10,000 from a firm of woolbrokers. The assets of the meatpackers were put up for security and they agreed that they would give the woolbrokers the right of first refusal on all its sheepskins and to pay commission on any sold to a third party for the five years of the loan. This would be the case even if the loan had been repaid since the borrowers had been given the right to repay at any time. One further term included was that the lenders agreed not to call in the loan at any time during five years. The borrowers challenged the term giving the right of first refusal to the woolbrokers.

The House of Lords upheld the term even though it was included in the mortgage terms. It concluded that it was not a clog or fetter on redemption.

 Jones v Morgan [2002] 1 EGLR 125

Morgan procured a loan from Jones to be secured on land which Morgan was interested in and on which he wished to develop housing. The loan was later varied to include a term that Morgan would transfer to Jones without payment of any price a one-half interest in the land. No order for specific performance was made.

It was held that although the subsequent variation was made three years after the loan it was held to be part of the original mortgage transaction. A provision that the mortgagor 'should have a share or interest in the mortgaged property' constituted an impermissible clog on the mortgagor's equity of redemption and could not be enforced.

12.1.2 The right to redeem must be preserved

PC *Fairclough v Swan Brewery Co Ltd* [1912] AC 565

A very long lease of a public house was mortgaged on terms that it could not be redeemed until six weeks before the lease expired, which was in 172 years' time!

The Privy Council held that this term was a fetter on redemption because it made the right to redeem the mortgage virtually worthless as the final six weeks would have practically no value.

CA *Knightsbridge Estates Trust Ltd v Byrne* [1939] Ch 441

A company had mortgaged its freehold property on terms that the mortgage would be repaid over a period of 40 years. The mortgagors wanted to redeem the mortgage early but the mortgagees objected.

The term postponing redemption was upheld and the mortgagees had no right to redeem early. The term was enforceable because it had been agreed between two businessmen as a commercial arrangement. If the property had been domestic property then it was unlikely that it would have been upheld.

12.1.3 The right to seek an order for sale against the wishes of the mortgagee

 Barrett v Halifax Building Society (1996) 28 HLR 634

The mortgagors had purchased their home with a mortgage. The property market had fallen and the value of the property had fallen below the original value (negative equity). They sought the right to sell rather than wait until the market rose in value.

The court was prepared to grant such an order as there was no discernible advantage in delaying sale. Section 91(2) LPA 1925 allowed the court the discretion to order sale at the request of the mortgagors.

12.1.4 Unfair terms

 Multiservice Bookbinding Ltd v Marden [1979] Ch 84

A mortgage had tied the interest and capital to a foreign currency. As a result of devaluation the repayments increased substantially. The mortgagor also agreed to pay interest at 2 per cent above the minimum lending rate. Over the four-year period the repayments of capital and interest amounted to nearly four times the amount borrowed. The mortgagor sought to have the loan set aside.

The court refused to set this aside because there was no evidence that the parties were in unequal bargaining positions, nor had one side tried to take advantage of the other and the mortgagor had received independent advice.

HC *Cityland & Property (Holding) Ltd v Dabrah* [1968] Ch 166

A mortgage included a term that on default the whole sum would become due. In this mortgage this meant a sum of £4,553, although £2,900 had been lent initially. The mortgagor had difficulties within a year and the full sum became payable. This represented 157 per cent of the loan and an annual interest rate of 38 per cent.

The court did not uphold the term because it was unfair, but instead substituted an interest rate of 7 per cent.

CA *Paragon Finance plc v Nash* [2002] 1 WLR 685

A challenge was made to the power inserted conventionally into a mortgage that there would be discretion to vary interest rates. Such a power would usually be reserved to take account of any variation in interest rates.

In this case the rate had been raised for a borrower because of losses incurred by the lender and this was held not to be unreasonable. The right to vary interest rates can be reserved but it should not be exercised 'dishonestly, for an improper purpose, capriciously or arbitrarily'. Examples were given where the rate of interest might be exercised for totally improper reasons, eg the bank manager did not like the colour of the borrower's hair.

12.1.5 The right to grant leases

 Barclays Bank plc v Zaroovabli **[1997] Ch 321**

A bank took a charge by way of legal mortgage over property
with registered title had failed to enter the charge on the
register as required. The charge contained a prohibition on
creating leases on the mortgagor. In breach of this provision
the mortgagor granted a lease for six months to a tenant who
became a statutory tenant under the Rent Act 1977.

The Court of Appeal held that this lease was binding on the
bank as an overriding interest. The lease took priority to the
charge which was only effect in equity until it was entered on
the register whereas the lease took effect in law and thereby
had priority.

12.1.6 Undue influence

The court have not been prepared to set aside a mortgage
simply because there has been inequality of bargaining power.
In *Lloyds Bank v Bundy* [1975] QB 326 Lord Denning had
unsuccessfully argued this principle. The House of Lords in
the later case of *National Westminster Bank v Morgan* [1985]
AC 686 said that as a court of conscience the court must
decide each case on its particular facts before deciding whether
there has been unconscionability.

HL *Barclays Bank v O'Brien* [1994] 1 AC 180

Mrs O'Brien signed a deed believing that she had secured a loan of £60,000 for her husband's failing business. In fact she had given the bank unlimited guarantee over the family home, which amounted to over £135,000 – double the amount she had agreed to. She had never been given independent advice from a solicitor on the effect of the document that she was signing and she had signed the document in front of a bank clerk and she had not properly read the document before signing. When the bank tried to gain possession of the house she argued that she had signed the documents as a result of her husband's undue influence.

The rights of a claimant, usually a wife, will prevail over the lender where the wife enters into a mortgage as a result of undue influence.

Undue influence can be either:

i) actual undue influence. Where the other party has actually exerted undue influence causing the claimant to enter into the transaction;

ii) presumed undue influence. Where the claimant does not have to show that there is actual undue influence but there is a relationship of trust and confidence between the claimant and the wrongdoer and the wrongdoer abused that relationship by procuring the claimant to enter into the transaction. Sometimes this confidential relationship is presumed, eg between solicitor and client. Sometimes it is for the claimant to prove that such a relationship existed.

HL *CIBC Mortgages plc v Pitt* **[1994] 1 AC 200**

Mr and Mrs Pitt jointly owned their matrimonial home and had an outstanding mortgage. Mr Pitt decided to take out a further loan. He told his wife that he wanted to do so because he wanted to invest in shares on the stock market. The loan was agreed with CIBC who lent £150,000 to them. Mrs Pitt did not read any of the documentation. The shares were purchased and at first they increased in value but after the stock market crash of 1987 they fell in value and Mr Pitt was unable to repay the loan. Mrs Pitt claimed that she had been subject to undue influence from her husband and therefore she had not fully understood the effect of the loan.

Both the Court of Appeal and the House of Lords agreed that Mr Pitt had exercised undue influence over his wife but that was not enough to fix the lenders with this undue influence. Mr Pitt was not acting as agent for CIBC.

HL *Royal Bank of Scotland plc v Etridge (No. 2)*
[1998] 4 All ER 705

A house had been purchased in the name of Mrs Etridge but Mr Etridge had provided the money. She later took out a loan of £100,000 to provide an overdraft facility for her husband's company. The first house was sold and a new house was purchased carrying the loan of £100,000. When the husband got into financial difficulties and the bank claimed the right to sell the house the wife argued that the loan should be set aside for undue influence.

The wife could not claim that she had been subject to undue influence. She had not been bullied by her husband and made to agree to take out the loan. However, the court held that there could be undue influence even where there had been independent advice.

Lord Nicholls
'In the normal course, advice from a solicitor or other outside adviser can be expected to bring home to a complainant a proper understanding of what he or she is about to do. But a person may understand fully the implications of a proposed transaction ... and yet be acting under the undue influence of another.'

The House of Lords continued to review the situations where the mortgagee may be affixed with constructive notice of the undue influence. It concluded that the mere fact that a mortgagee is put on inquiry that a mortgagor might be involved in a transaction subject to undue influence does not inevitably mean that the mortgage will be set aside. The mortgagee must take reasonable steps to ensure that the mortgagor was not acting under the undue influence of a third party.

Lord Nicholls
'For the future, a bank satisfies these requirements if it insists that the wife attend a private meeting with a representative of the bank at which she is told of the extent of her liability as surety, warned of the risk she is running and urged to take independent legal advice. In exceptional cases the bank, to be safe, has to insist that the wife is separately advised.'

Alliance & Leicester plc v Slayford [2001] 1 All ER (Comm) 1

The Building Society appealed against the dismissal of its application for leave to pursue a money judgment against the mortgagor. The mortgagor's wife successfully argued that she had signed the consent form without adequate advice and the possession proceedings against her were dismissed. The building society applied for leave to amend the pleadings to allow it to pursue a money judgment against the husband.

The Court of Appeal upheld the building society's right to amend the pleadings.

A mortgagee was not prevented from pursuing a different remedy following its failure to realise its security through possession proceedings even where such proceedings might result in an application by the trustee in bankruptcy for sale of the property.

12.2 Rights of the mortgagee

12.2.1 The right to possession

Four-Maids Ltd v Dudley Marshall [1957] Ch 317

Harman J
'... The mortgagee may go into possession before the ink is dry on the mortgage unless there is something in the contract, express or by implication whereby he has contracted himself out of that right ...'

The legal mortgagee's right to possession arises as soon as the mortgage is made (and even in advance of the date fixed for redemption)

 CA *Palk v Mortgage Services Funding plc* [1993] Ch 330

In this case the mortgagee was seeking possession of the mortgagor's house. The property had fallen in value due to a recession and the mortgagees wanted to retain the property and sell at a time when the property prices had risen in value. They wanted to let the house on lease during this time. The issue was whether they could do this and whether during this time the mortgagor still had to make payments due under the loan contract.

The mortgagor was held to remain liable for the mortgage repayments, however he had the power himself to ask the court to order sale. In this case the court ordered sale having been persuaded that to delay sale would have resulted in the debt growing impossibly large which the mortgagors would have had little prospect of ever repaying.

If the mortgagee forces a sale and the proceeds of sale do not meet the amount owing then the mortgagor remains liable on any outstanding amounts.

 CA *Quennell v Maltby* [1979] 1 All ER 568

The mortgagor had leased out the mortgaged premises which was not authorised by the mortgage deed. The mortgagor and his wife wanted to evict the tenants but were unable to do so in their capacity as mortgagor. When they discovered that they could do so in their capacity as mortgagees his wife decided to pay off the mortgage and then after transfer of the mortgage seek possession as mortgagee.

The mortgagee was not *bona fide* exercising her rights as mortgagee in order to protect the security and so her claim for possession failed.

 Cheltenham and Gloucester Building Society v Norgan [1996] 1 WLR 343

In this case the mortgagor resisted an application for an order for possession by showing that repayments could be made over a long period of time but if it was restricted to two to four years, as was usual in such cases, then repayments would have been impossible.

Under s 36 Administration of Justice Act 1970 the courts have the right to adjourn possession proceedings relating to a dwelling house for such period as the court thinks reasonable, if it appears that the mortgagor may, within a reasonable period, be in a position to repay the sums due under the mortgage or to remedy a default. In this case the courts exercised their right to delay repayments of mortgage arrears by considering the whole period of the mortgage as opposed to ordering repayments within a shorter period of one or two years.

When considering what a reasonable period is, the starting point should be the whole length remaining of the mortgage. Once this has been established the court should look at whether or not the mortgagor could repay over the whole period.

The court must look at several key issues:

i) how much of the mortgage term remains?
ii) how much can the mortgagor reasonably afford to pay both now and in the future?
iii) why has the borrower been unable to pay and how long will this reason last? If the prospect of repayment is not reasonable then an order for possession will be made immediately.

 Cheltenham and Gloucester Building Society v Krausz
[1997] 1 All ER 21

A mortgagor sought an order for sale of a mortgaged property when the mortgagee had obtained a warrant for possession and had yet to execute that warrant. The proposed sale price would not have produced sufficient funds to discharge the amount owing. The Court of Appeal refused to order a sale and instead allowed the warrant for possession to be enforced.

Philips LJ
'... S 36 does not empower the court to suspend possession in order to permit the mortgagor to sell the mortgaged premises where the proceeds of sale will not suffice to discharge the mortgage debt, unless of course other funds will be available to the mortgagor to make up the shortfall ...'

First National Bank v Syed [1991] 2 All ER 250

A court must look at the mortgagor's financial position realistically.

A court should not sanction the postponement of a possession order unless it is based upon a realistic assessment of the situation. It should neither make an order which would clear the arrears and meet the ongoing payments if it is one that the mortgagor cannot afford nor alternatively make an order which the mortgagor could afford but would not within a reasonable time enable the arrears to be cleared.

CA ### *Target Homes v Clothier* [1994] 1 All ER 439

In most cases where the mortgagee applies for sale the court will grant it and the mortgagor will have no right to sell himself. In this case the mortgagor brought evidence to court from an estate agent that the property could be sold by the mortgagor. He even showed that there had been offers for the property. The offer would cover all the arrears in payments and the loan.

In the circumstances the court were prepared to defer sale because there was clearly a good prospect of sale. This was unusual because once an order for possession was granted then usually the mortgagees would take decisions on sale. The order for possession was deferred for three months.

12.2.2 The right to sell

AIB Finance v Debtors AC [1998] 2 All ER 929

The mortgagors ran a shop as a post office, newsagent and off-licence. They took out a mortgage but could not repay the instalments and the mortgagees repossessed the property and sold it after six months. The mortgagors argued that the mortgagees had not preserved the business sufficiently over the six months before sale and this had resulted in a lower price than expected.

The mortgagees did not owe a duty to the mortgagors prior to taking possession in this case because the mortgagors themselves had taken certain actions which had affected their viability as a business such as selling the newspaper round to another business. However, generally the law puts a duty on the mortgagees to preserve a business if it is a going concern before its sale.

Cuckmere Brick Co Ltd v Mutual Finance Ltd [1971] Ch 949

Property was sold at what the mortgagor regarded at undervalue and the mortgagor sued the mortgagee alleging that the sale price achieved was too low. The mortgagor argued that the fact that there was planning permission attached to the land was not properly advertised. The majority of the Court of Appeal held that the mortgagee's duty to the mortgagor had been broken.

Skipton Building Society v Stott [2000] 2 All ER 779

The mortgagee sold the mortgaged property to an adjoining landowner and did not first offer it on the open market. The amount owed by the mortgagor was less than the market value so the mortgagor did not owe any further sum to the mortgagee.

12.2.3 Appointment of a receiver

 Medforth v Blake [1999] 3 All ER 97

A receiver took over a pig farming business after the farmer could not repay instalments on the loan to the business. The farmer argued that the receiver had not managed the business properly as he had failed to get discounts on pig feed which were available. Since this was the major expense of the business he reduced its profitability.

The receiver owes a duty of due diligence to the mortgagor over management of the premises. It is not just a duty of good faith but can cover practical issues in the day-to-day running of the business. A receiver may choose not to continue to run a business but if the receiver does choose to continue to run the business previously run by the mortgagor then duties are owed by the mortgagee in the management of the business.

12.2.4 Foreclosure

This is a draconian remedy and is rarely sought and rarely granted today.

It was not sought by the mortgagee in *Palk v Mortgage Services Funding* (above) who preferred to seek possession.

The Law Commission has recommended that it should be abolished.

THE NATURE OF A LEASE

Bruton v London & Quadrant Housing Trust (2000)
A lease can exist in law even where the landlord has no legal title to the land
Street v Mountford (1985)
A lease has these features: exclusive possession; for a fixed term and at a rent
i) A term
Lace v Chantler (1944)
The period of the lease must be certain
Prudential Assurance Co Ltd v London Residuary Body (1992)
Where land is retained until the owner requires it back no lease can exist because the term is uncertain
ii) At a rent
Ashburn Anstalt v Arnold (1989)
A tenancy can exist without the payment of rent
iii) Exclusive possession
Somma v Hazelhurst (1978)
The intention of the parties indicates whether a lease is created
Street v Mountford (1985)
Overruling *Somma v Hazelhurst* a tenancy exists if the key features: rent; exclusive possession and a fixed term exist
Aslan v Murphy (1990)
A sham device giving rights of entry to the landlord will not prevent a tenancy from arising
Antoniades v Villiers (1990)
Retention of a right to live in the premises by the landlord will not prevent exclusive possession if the term is deemed to be a 'sham'
A-G Securities v Vaughan (1990)
Enjoyment of joint facilities under separate agreements gave rise to separate licences

REMEDIES
SPECIFIC PERFORMANCE OF A COVENANT

Jeune v Queens Cross Properties Ltd (1974)
Rainbow Estates Ltd v Tokenhold (1999)
Both tenants and landlords can be awarded specific performance of a covenant in a lease

FORFEITURE

Billson v Residential Apartments Ltd (1992)
In most cases a tenant has the right to seek relief from forfeiture where the landlord has re-entered the premises

WAIVER

Central Estates (Belgravia) v Woolgar (1972)
Acceptance of rent after breach constitutes waiver of rights by the landlord

13.1 The nature of a lease

Bruton v London and Quadrant Housing Trust
[2000] 1 AC 406

A housing trust had been granted a licence to use properties as temporary shelter for the homeless. The properties were to be developed. The trust undertook that they would not allow any of the occupiers to become tenants without prior consent of the Council. Mr B signed an agreement with the trust that he would occupy a self-contained flat in one of these buildings on a temporary basis on a weekly licence. Under the agreement he was to vacate the premises upon reasonable notice from the trust. After six years he claimed that he had a lease by estoppel.

A lease had been granted to Mr Bruton. He had all the key features of a tenant rather than a licensee – in particular the trust had to give him notice to vacate the premises.

The interesting feature of this case is that the lease could be granted even though the trust did not have legal title to the land. This has caused considerable criticism because the tenancy will take effect in law and could be enforced against third party purchasers but the trust who granted him the right to live there could not themselves claim a proprietary right in the land.

13.2 The difference between a lease and a licence

HL *Street v Mountford* [1985] AC 809

 An agreement was drawn up between the parties, Mr Street and Mrs Mountford. It was called a licence but it had many of the key features of a tenancy – in particular the licensee had exclusive possession of the premises. Mrs Mountford claimed protection under the Rent Acts.

 The House of Lords found that a tenancy had been created. The court adopted an objective approach to the agreement and found that Mrs Mountford had the right to live in the property with;

   i) exclusive possession;

   ii) for a term;

   iii) at a rent.

The court concluded that these were the key features of a tenancy.

 Lord Templeman
'If the agreement satisfied all the requirements of a tenancy, then the agreement produced a tenancy and the parties cannot alter the effect of the agreement by insisting that they only created a licence. The manufacture of a five-pronged implement for digging results in a fork even if the manufacturer, unfamiliar with the English language, insists that he intended to make and has made a spade.'

13.3 Key features of a lease

13.3.1 The period must be certain

CA | *Lace v Chantler* [1944] KB 368

A tenant of a house granted a sub-lease to the defendant during the Second World War for 'the duration of the war'.

The term was uncertain and therefore did not create a good leasehold interest. A lease will not take effect if it is impossible to say at the outset how long it will last. This prevents the possibility that a lease will last forever and so deprive the freehold owner of any rights.

HL | *Prudential Assurance Co Ltd v London Residuary Body* [1992] 2 AC 386

An agreement had been made between the London County Council and the owner of a strip of land fronting the highway. The owner sold it to the Council but in return leased it back on terms that it should continue 'until the land is required by the Council ... for the purpose of widening the highway'.

The term was uncertain and so, following *Lace v Chantler*, there could not be a lease of the land.

Lord Templeman

'A lease can be made for five years subject to the tenant's right to determine if the war ends before the expiry of five years. A lease can be made from year to year subject to a fetter on the right of the landlord to determine the lease before the expiry of five years unless the war ends. Both leases are valid because they create a determinable certain term of years. A lease might purport to be made for the duration of the war subject to the tenant's right to determine before the end of the war ... A term must either be certain or uncertain. It cannot be partly certain because the tenant can determine it at any time and partly uncertain because the landlord cannot determine it for an uncertain period.'

13.3.2 The payment of rent

CA *Ashburn Anstalt v Arnold* [1989] Ch 1

An agreement was concluded between the parties that the claimants would have rights to enjoy land for a term but without the payment of rent.

The Court of Appeal concluded that a tenancy could take effect even where the parties did not pay rent in spite of Lord Templeman's judgment in *Street v Mountford*.

Section 205(1)(xxvii) LPA 1925 defines a term of years absolute without referring to the need for rent; indeed, it expressly says that 'a term of years ... taking effect either in possession or in reversion whether or not for rent'.

13.3.3 Exclusive possession

AC *Somma v Hazelhurst* [1978] 1 WLR 1014

A young married couple moved into a double bed-sitting room for which they paid weekly rent. The landlord did not provide services to them such as meals or bed linen or cleaning. The agreement reserved the right to the landlord to move in himself or to move in anyone he wished to live in the premises with them.

The fact that the parties called the agreement a licence was conclusive and the features that suggested it was a lease were less important than the intention of the parties. This case was overruled in *Street v Mountford* (1985).

HL *Street v Mountford* [1985] AC 809

This case turned on the fact that Mrs Mountford had exclusive possession of the premises. It was decided that it was this feature that would distinguish a lease from a licence.

Would it be possible today, after *Street v Mountford*, to enter into a licence that had the features of a tenancy? If not, has this affected parties' freedom in relation to leases and licences?

CA *Aslan v Murphy* [1990] 1 AC 417

Property was let on terms that the owner would retain keys and enjoy the absolute right to enter at all times. It was called a licence. The owner also inserted a term requiring the claimant to vacate the premises for an hour and a half each day.

This agreement was a tenancy. The terms retaining the right of entry for the landlord and requiring the premises to be vacated each day were 'sham devices' which was inserted in order to prevent the agreement from becoming a lease. The court also thought that the retention of keys did not prevent the agreement from becoming a tenancy in law.

HL *Westminster City Council v Clarke* [1992] 2 AC 288

The council ran a hostel for the homeless and retained the right to be able to move someone from one room to another at any time. It was held that this prevented any of the residents from claiming that he had a tenancy since he did not have exclusive possession.

Lord Templeman
'… in the circumstances of the present case I consider that the Council legitimately and effectively retained for themselves possession of room E and that Mr Clarke was only a licensee with rights corresponding to the rights of a lodger.

HL *Antoniades v Villiers* [1990] 1 AC 417

A couple occupied premises jointly and had exclusive occupation. The two had signed separate agreements which reserved the right of the landlord to go into occupation of the flat or to move others into the flat. The agreements were called licences.

The agreements took effect as leases. The insertion of terms allowing the landlord to move himself or others in were purely there as a sham in order to prevent the lease from taking effect at law.

 ### A-G Securities v Vaughan [1990] 1 AC 417

The House of Lords found that where four people shared a flat as independent occupiers then their agreements could be seen as separate licences for each occupier. Each occupier had joint use of the bathroom, kitchen and the sitting room but they had sole use of their bedrooms.

Each tenant enjoyed rights as licensees only. If this were a joint tenancy in law, then if one person died the remaining tenants would assume the legal tenancy until eventually there would be only one left.

13.4 Remedies

13.4.1 Specific performance of a covenant

Both the tenant and the landlord can seek specific performance of a covenant in a lease but it is most unusual for the court to award it. The tenant was granted specific performance of a repairing covenant in *Jeune v Queens Cross Properties Ltd* [1974] Ch 97. This right was extended to landlords in *Rainbow Estates Ltd v Tokenhold* [1999] Ch 64. This is unusual and it is thought more appropriate for the court to award forfeiture.

13.4.2 Forfeiture

 Billson v Residential Apartments Ltd [1992] 1 AC 494

The defendant tenants had broken a term in their agreement that they would not alter the premises or assign the lease without consent of the landlords. After prolonged negotiations the landlords peaceably forced their way into the premises and changed the locks of the premises. Later the tenants regained possession. The judge at first instance refused the tenants the right to gain relief from forfeiture.

A tenant has a right to seek relief from forfeiture where the landlord has re-entered the premises in all cases except where the case comes within the jurisdiction of the County Courts Act 1984 which lays down a time-limit of six months.

13.4.3 Waiver

 Central Estates (Belgravia) Ltd v Woolgar (No 2) [1972] 1 WLR 1048

The landlords sought to recover property after the tenant had been in breach of covenant, but they had accepted payments in rent and the tenant argued that they had waived their right to enforce the covenant.

The landlords had waived their rights. There were unusual facts here, the breach had been temporary, the premises had not been damaged and the tenant had been elderly and not in good health.

CHAPTER 14

ADVERSE POSSESSION

MEANING OF 'ADVERSE POSSESSION'
Red House Farms (Thorndon) Ltd v Catchpole (1977)
Evidence of factual possession depends on the type of land

FACTUAL POSSESSION
Tecbild v Chamberlain (1969)
Trivial acts of trespass do not constitute factual possession of land
Boosey v Davis (1987)
Trivial, intermittent or equivocal acts will not be sufficient as evidence of factual possession

INTENTION TO POSSESS
Lambeth LBC v Blackburn (2001)
Powell v Macfarlane (1977)
Adverse possession involves proof of intention to exclude all others including the owner from the land
Bucks County Council v Moran (1990)
Intention to possess is not an intention to own the property
Pye v Graham (2001)
The intention to possess is not undermined where the squatter admits they would have paid for the right to occupy

HUMAN RIGHTS
Pye (JA) (Oxford) Ltd v UK (2008)
The Grand Chamber of the European Court of Human Rights concluded that the law on adverse possession in UK law both pre- and post-the LRA 2002 was not contrary to human rights
Ofulue v Bossert [2008] 3 WLR 1253
A landowner cannot challenge a successful application for adverse possession on the basis of Article One Protocol One of the ECHR

LAWFUL POSSESSION
BP Properties v Buckler (1987)
Time ceases to run once a person is offered a lawful right to be on the property

LEASEHOLD PROPERTY
St Marylebone Property Co Ltd v Fairweather (1963)
A squatter can be evicted by a landlord in unregistered land even after the tenant has been dispossessed. The rule is different in registered land

14.1 Meaning of 'adverse possession'

CA *Red House Farms (Thorndon) Ltd v Catchpole*
[1977] 2 EGLR 125

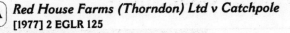

The squatter based his claim over land on evidence of shooting over the land. It was marshy and unsuitable for growing crops or grazing animals. Access was limited as a bridge had collapsed. It was accepted that shooting alone was proof of factual possession.

The claimant must show evidence of factual possession. This will depend on the type of land. If the land is unsuitable for all but very limited infrequent use then this may be sufficient evidence of factual possession.

HC *RB Policies at Lloyd's v Butler* **[1950] 1 KB 76**

Streatfield J
'(T)hose who go to sleep upon their claims should not be assisted by the courts recovering their property, but another, and I think equal policy behind the Acts is that there shall be an end to litigation.'

14.2 Factual possession

CA *Tecbild v Chamberlain* **(1969) 20 P & CR 633**

The claimant failed to persuade the court that allowing his children to play on land and to tether and exercise their ponies constituted acts of factual possession.

The acts were held to be merely trivial acts of trespass.

CA *Boosey v Davis* (1987) 55 P& CR 83

The claimant had cleared an area of scrub and put livestock on the land and even erected a fence. This was not sufficient to support a claim for adverse possession since it could not be said that the owner had himself been dispossessed. The fencing erected was merely a reinforcement of the original fence erected by the owner. The grazing of the animals was intermittent.

Any act which is found to be trivial, intermittent or equivocal will not be sufficient as evidence of factual possession.

14.3 Intention to possess

HC *Powell v Macfarlane* (1977) 38 P & CR 452

A 14-year-old boy started grazing his cow on some vacant land. He did this intermittently for some years as well as cutting a hay crop, carrying out repairs to the boundary fence, cutting back undergrowth and connecting a rudimentary water supply system. He added a goat and other cows to the land. However, the judge did not think that that was sufficient evidence of an intention to possess. In particular he did not think that someone so young could form such an intention.

Adverse possession involves proof of an intention to possess and that meant the claimant must intend to exclude all others from the land, including the owner.

Slade J
'(T)he courts will … require clear and affirmative evidence that the trespasser, claiming that he has acquired possession, not only had the requisite intention to possess, but made such an intention clear to the world.'

CA *Bucks County Council v Moran* [1990] Ch 623

A local authority had acquired land for future road development. This was incorporated into the garden of one of the neighbouring landowners. Bulbs were planted, hedges were trimmed, the grass was cut and a fence was erected around it. Later a gate was put into the fence, secured by a lock and chain that prevented access by anyone but the squatter. These acts were sufficient to constitute acts of factual possession.

The court did not accept the local authority's claim that the squatter was aware of the future plans for the plot and this prevented him from forming an intention to possess the land.

Adverse possession is based on an intention to possess. It does not require proof of an intention to own or even an intention to own in the future. Knowledge of plans for future use of the land does not prevent a squatter from successfully claiming possession so long as there is very clear evidence of possessory acts and intentions.

HL *JA Pye (Oxford) Ltd v Graham* [2001] Ch 804

 The defendants had farmed land over a period of years under licence from the claimants. The acts included grazing large numbers of cattle, caring for the land by ploughing and applying fertiliser; trimming the hedges every year and maintenance of all fences and ditches. After the licence expired the defendants requested a further licence but the claimants refused this. The defendants remained in occupation and the claimants ignored subsequent requests for a further licence. The court held that the continued acts were adverse to the owner and the defendants successfully claimed rights over the land under the pre-Land Registration Act 2002 rules.

 It was held that the adverse possessor need only prove intention to possess and not an intention to own the land. This intention would not be undermined where the adverse possessor admitted that he would have been prepared to pay the owner for a license to occupy the land.

 Neuberger J
'It is hard to see what principle of justice entitles the trespasser to acquire the land for nothing from the owner simply because he has been permitted to remain there for 12 years.' (At first instance.)

 Lord Browne-Wilkinson
'There will be a "dispossession" of the paper owner in any case where … a squatter assumes possession in the ordinary sense of the word. Except in the case of joint possessors, possession is single and exclusive. Therefore if the squatter is in possession the paper owner cannot be. If the paper owner was

> at one stage in possession of the land but the
> squatter's subsequent occupation of it in law
> constitutes possession the squatter must have
> dispossessed the true owner.'

CA *Lambeth LBC v Blackburn* (2001) 82 P & CR 39

A squatter appealed against an order for possession by the local
authority claiming that he had had possession for 12 years.
The local authority maintained that he had not shown the
requisite intention to possess. The squatter had first entered
the property by force breaking the lock but he had installed
his own lock and gradually improved the property.

His claim was upheld. The fact that he expected to be evicted
at any time did not prevent him from having that intention.

CA *BP Properties v Buckler* (1987) 55 P & CR 337

Mrs Buckler was sent a letter by the owner of the property
offering her a licence to occupy. She did not respond to the
letter as she believed that she had a lawful right to be on the
premises. The licence was binding on Mrs Buckler and once
she received the offer time ceased to run against the legal title
owner of the land.

Time will cease to run in favour of a person in adverse
possession once they are offered a lawful right to be on the
property, either through a licence or a lease. Time will only
continue to run if the offer is refused, not if it is simply ignored.

14.4 Adverse possession of leasehold property

HL *St Marylebone Property Co Ltd v Fairweather* [1963] AC 510

A squatter had dispossessed a tenant of property for a period of 12 years and was entitled to occupy under the lease until it expired. The tenant voluntarily surrendered his lease to the landlord who then had the right to recover his property from the squatter.

Traditionally, the law was applied differently in cases of adverse possession against a tenant according to whether it was registered or unregistered land. In unregistered land cases the landlord retains the right to recover the land against the squatter whereas in registered land, recovery of the land against the squatter is delayed until the original lease has expired. Then the rights of the squatter end because they only acquire the rights of the tenant whom they dispossessed and not the legal estate vested in the landlord: *Spectrum Investment v Holmes* [1981] 1 WLR 221.

14.5 Human rights

In 2005 Pye ltd took their case to the European Court of Human rights. They claimed that art 1 and Protocol One of the European Convention on Human Rights had been breached by the law on adverse possession in the UK. The court found in its favour by a majority of four votes to three and ordered the UK government to pay compensation to Pye Ltd. The UK government appealed to the Grand Chamber of the European Court of Appeal.

Pye (JA)(Oxford) Ltd v UK (2008) 46 EHRR 1083

The Grand Chamber by a majority of ten votes to seven overturned the earlier finding. The law on adverse possession in the UK, both the Land Registration Act 2002 and the Land Registration Act 1925, was compatible with human rights. The court found that the balance between the individual owner's peaceful enjoyment of his possessions and the demands of the public interest was maintained. The court also held that limitation period pursued a legitimate aim in the general interest. They held that the paper owner in Pye must have been aware of the statutory limitation principle and was not without procedural protection.

CA ### *Ofulue v Bossert* [2008] 3 WLR 1253

Mr Ofulue purchased some property in England which he let to tenants before returning to live in Nigeria. In 1981 the tenant let the claimant Mr Bossert and his daughter into the property and they started to carry out improvements to it. Mr Ofulue returned from Nigeria from time to time and asked them to leave but he did not pursue proceedings to recover the property from them. In 2000 possession proceedings were brought against them. These were dismissed and fresh proceedings were brought in 2003. The court found that time had run against the owner and upheld the claim of adverse possession by the claimants.

The Court of Appeal dismissed a claim by the owner that his human rights had been violated under art 1 Protocol One. The court applied *Pye v UK* and held that it should be followed unless there were exceptional reasons for not following it and there were no such reasons here.

CA *Ofulue v Bossert* **[2009] 2 WLR 749**

A further appeal by the landowner was dismissed. The landowner claimed that time ceased to run when the squatter made an offer to buy the property. The offer had been refused and time did not cease to run.

The decision in *Pye v UK* effectively prevents any landowner from pleading violation of his human rights as a defence to a claim by a squatter. The only possibility of pleading human rights would be to show that there are exceptional circumstances.

INDEX

access to land 3, 5
    easements 26, 108–111
Access to Neighbouring Land Act 1992 3
actual occupation 30–33
Administration of Justice Act 1970
    142–143
advancement, resulting trusts 43–47
adverse possession 158–159
    factual possession 159–160
    and human rights 164–166
    intention to possess 160–163
    leasehold property 164
    time limits 162–166
airspace above land, ownership 1–4
alienation 88–89
annexation
    chattels 11–14
    covenants 123–126
    degree and purpose, tests for 11–15
    fixtures and fittings 11–16

bankruptcy 46, 89, 99–101
below surface, ownership 5, 9–10
beneficial interests 40, 47–49, 78–80
breach, restrictive covenant 127–128
building schemes, covenants 125–126
burdens, reciprocal 69–70
business partners 40, 82–83

chattels
    annexation 11–14
    buried 9–10
    lost, rights over 5–8
    in or attached to land 6–8
    stolen 7–8
children, rights of 34
clogs or fetters 130–132
co-ownership, of land/ property 59, 81, 92
    see also joint tenancies
    assessment of share of 54–59
    business partners 82–83
    and constructive trusts 49–52, 56–57

express declaration of 82–83
    resulting trusts 39–42, 46, 58–59
cohabitees, rights of 49–52
common intention
    constructive trusts 40, 48–59
    implied easements 112–113
common law
    proprietary interests in land 20–22
    severance of joint tenancy 87–89
compensation, grant of 69
consideration 25
constructive trusts 20, 33, 37–38
    assessment of share of 54–59
    beneficial interests 40, 47–49, 78–80
    common intention 48–59
    contractual licences 73–80
    unregistered right 17, 20–21, 36
continuous use, easements 114
contracts
    exchange of 17–19
    variation 19
    in writing 18–19
contractual licences
    constructive trusts 73–80
    and estoppel 71, 76
    proprietary status 77–80
contrary intention 58–59
conveyancing 14
    unregistered land 23–27
    voluntary 41–42
covenants 117–120
    annexation 123–126
    building schemes 125–126
    burden of 70, 121–124
    in equity 121–125
    at law 118–121
    positive 70, 121–124
    restrictive 119, 122–123
        breach of 127–128
    specific performance 155–156
    successors in title 89, 109, 120,
        122–123, 126

touching and concerning land
118–119, 122
Crown rights 5

detrimental reliance 66–68
doctrines
lost modern grant 114–115
notice 23
survivorship 88
dominant tenements, rights of 105–106,
123

easements 103–105
access/ rights of way 26, 108–111
burden of 109
common intention 112–113
equitable 29
excessive use 115–116
implied 111–112
and licences 105–106
lost modern grant, doctrine of
114–115
necessity 113–114
parking rights 107–108
under prescription 107, 114–115
restrictions on 106–109
right to quiet enjoyment 2–4,
104–106, 111–112, 165
subject matter of 106–109
Wheeldon v Burrows, rule in 110–111
equitable interests in land 32–35, 78–79,
92
equity
covenants 121–125
equitable interests in land 32–35,
–78–79, 92
estoppel *see also* proprietary estoppel
licences 71, 76
European Convention on Human Rights
1950 100, 164–166
excessive use, easements 115–116
exchange of contracts 17–19
exclusive possession 153–155
express annexation, covenants 125
express trusts 82–83

factual possession 159–160
Family Law Act 1996 29–30
fetters 130–132
finder, rights of 5–10
'finders keepers' 5–8
five *probanda* 61–62

fixtures and fittings 1
annexation 11–15
chattels 11–14
everyday objects 15
tenant's fixtures 15–16
test for 11–14
trade fixtures 16
foreclosure 147
forfeiture
joint tenancies 89–90
leases 156
Forfeiture Act 1982 90
fraud
and equity 48
transfer of joint tenancy 87–89

garden ornaments 15–16
'gazumping' 18
good faith 25–26, 34–36

human rights 44, 100, 164–166

illegal purpose, resulting trusts 41–42,
44–46
implied easements 111–112
injunctions 2–3, 127–128
Insolvency Act 1986 99–100
intention
adverse possession 160–163
constructive trusts 40, 48–59
contrary intention 58–59
implied easements 112–113
leases 153–155
resulting trusts 43–47
interests, in land
beneficial 40, 47–49, 78–80
equitable 32–35, 78–79, 92
land charges 23–27
and licences 71–73
overriding, and occupation 27, 30–33
proprietary 20–22
items found in/ on land
buried 9–10
lost 5–8

joint ownership, of land *see* co-ownership
joint tenancies 155
alienation 88–89
forfeiture 89–90
fraudulent transfer 87–89
severance
at common law 83, 87–89

by post 84–87
by statute 83–84
tenancies in common 82, 98

land, defining 1–4
land charges 23–27
Land Charges Act 1972 23
Land Registration Act 1925 25, 30, 165
Land Registration Act 2002 26, 30,
34–35, 165
Land Registry 29–30
Law of Property Act 1925
annexation of covenants 124
and constructive trusts 48
implied easements 111–112
order for sale 134
and overreaching 101–102
and resulting trusts 41–42
severance of joint tenancies under
83–84
term of lease and rent 152
Law of Property (Miscellaneous Provisions)
Act 1989 19, 21, 42
law reform
co-habitees 44, 54
foreclosure 147
leasehold property 9
adverse possession 164
leases 148–149
exclusive possession 153–155
features of 149–155
intention 153–155
and licences 77, 150, 153–155
mortgagor's right to grant 136
remedies, for breach 155–157
rent 97–98, 152
sham devices 153–155
term of 151–152
licences 71
contractual 73–80
and easements 105–106
and estoppel 71, 76
and interests/ grants 71–73
and leases 77, 150, 153–155
and third parties 76–80
trespass 72–74
loans 46–47, 132 *see also* mortgages
lock-out agreements 17–18
locus in quo 8
lost items, rights over 5–8
lost modern grant, doctrine of 114–115

Matrimonial Causes Act 1973 54
Matrimonial Homes Acts 1967 and 1983
30
matrimonial rights 26–27, 29–30, 39–42,
75–76, 78
mines, gold and silver 5
mistake 60–61
mortgagee, rights of 77, 130, 147
annexation of covenants 125
appointment of receiver 146
possession 140–144
to sell 145–146
mortgages 129–130
foreclosure 147
order for sale 134
redemption 130–133
unfair terms 134–135
and unregistered interests in land
26–27
mortgagor, rights of 129–140
to grant leases 136
order for sale 134
redemption 130–133
undue influence 129, 136–140
unfair terms 134–135

necessity, implied easements 113–114
neighbouring land 3
notice, doctrine of 23
postal delivery 84–87
nuisance 4

occupation
actual 30–33
grant of right to 69
and overriding interests 27, 30–33
occupiers
overriding interests 30–31
rights and liabilities 6–7
option to purchase, void 19
order for sale 99–101, 134, 145–146
overreaching 101–102
overriding interests 29–36
actual occupation 30–33
children 34
good faith 34–36
occupiers 27
temporary absences 34
owner, true 162–163
ownership of land *see also* co-ownership
airspace above 1–4
below surface 5, 9–10

parking rights 107–108
positive covenants 70, 121–124
possession *see also* adverse possession
    exclusive 153–155
    intention 160–163
post, severance of tenancy by 85–87
postal delivery 84–87
prescription, easements under 107,
        114–115
presumption
    advancement 43–47
    resulting trusts 39–42
probanda, five 61–62
proprietary estoppel 17, 20–21, 60
    and claimant's misconduct 70
    definition 61–62
    five *probanda* 61–62
    proportionality 68–70
    reliance 62–68
        detrimental 66–68
    remedies 68–70
    representation 62–68
proprietary rights/ interests, in land 20–22
    and licences 71–73
purchase money 39
    contributions to, and constructive
            trusts 51–59
purchaser
    rights 36
    unprotected interests 36

quiet enjoyment, right to 2–4, 104–106,
        111–112, 165

receiver, appointment of 130, 146
redemption, of mortgages 130–133
registered land 28
    adverse possession 158–163
    and good faith 34–35
    overriding interests 28–36
registration, of title 29–30
reliance 62–68
    detrimental 66–68
remedies
    breach of restrictive covenant 127–128
    injunctions 2–3, 127–128
    proportionality 68–69
    proprietary estoppel 68–70
    specific performance 155–156
rent 97–98 , 152
repairs 3–4, 97–98

representation 62–68
resulting trusts 37
    advancement of 43–47
    assessment of share of 54–59
    illegal purpose 41–42, 44–46
    intention 43–47
    loans 46–47
    presumption of 39–42
rights *see also* rights in land
    business partners 82–83
    children 34
    landowners 8–9
    leaseholders 9
    mortgagees 77, 125, 130, 140–147
    mortgagors 129–140
    occupiers 6–7
    parking 107–108
    personal 29–30, 80
    purchaser 36
    quiet enjoyment of property 2–4,
            104–106, 111–112, 165
    redemption, of mortgage 130–133
    to sale 130, 134, 145–146
    of spouse 26–27, 29–30, 39–42,
            49–54, 75–76, 78
    squatters 159–164
    superior 105–106, 123
rights in land
    common intention 40, 48–59,
            112–113
    prior to exchange of contracts 17–19
    rights of way 26, 108–111
    third parties 29–30, 80
    transfer 17–19, 20–22, 87–89
rights of way 26, 108–111

sale of land
    contracts in writing 18–19
    option to purchase, void 19
    order for 134
    right to sale 130, 134, 145–146
    rights prior to exchange of contracts
        17–19
    variation of contract terms 19
searches, land registration
    incorrect names 24–25
severance, of joint tenancies
    at common law 83, 87–89
    by post 84–87
    by statute 83–84
share in property, assessment of 54–59

specific performance 155–156
spouse, rights of 26–27, 29–30, 39–42,
    49–52, 75–76, 78
squatters 159–166
Standard Conditions of Sale 14
stolen property 7–8
successors in title 89, 109, 120, 122–123,
    126
Suicide Act 1961 90
superior rights 105–106, 123
survivorship, doctrine of 89

television reception 4
tenancies see also joint tenancies; leases
    tenancies in common 82, 98
tenant's fixtures 15–16
terms
    in leases 151–152
    unfair terms 134–135
    variation of 19
third parties
    licences 76–80
    personal rights of 29–30, 80
time limits, adverse possession 162–166
title to land
    registration of 29–30
    transfers in good faith 25
touching and concerning 118–119, 122
transfer of rights in land
    avoidance of formalities 17, 20–22
    contracts in writing 18–19
    fraudulent 87–89
    variation of contract terms 19
trespass
    adverse possession 159–164
    in airspace 2–4
    by digging 9–10
    licences 72–74
trusts see also constructive trusts; resulting
    trusts; trusts over land
    express 82–83
Trusts of Land and Appointment of
    Trustees Act 1996 92, 94–97
trusts over land 91–92
    and bankruptcy 99–101
    overreaching 101–102
    purpose of 93–95
    and sale of land, applications for
        96–101

uncertain terms, in leases 151–152
unconscionability 47, 136
undue influence 129, 136–140
unfair terms 134–135
unregistered land 23–27, 164
    transfers in good faith 25–26

variation, of contract 19

waiver, leases 156–157
Wheeldon v Burrows, rule in 110–111
Williams v Hensman, severance of tenancy
    under 87
writing, contracts in 18–19